DEFENCE APTITUDE ASSESSMENT

how2become.com

Orders: Please contact www.How2Become.com

ISBN: 9781912370924

First published in 2023 by How2Become Ltd.

Copyright © 2023 How2Become. All rights reserved.

Disclaimer:

IMPORTANT: All resources, products, content, and training from How2Become is intended for educational use only, as an aid to help you prepare and come up with your own honest answers. How2Become is not acting in conjunction with, or associated with, any third-party organisation.

How2Become and its sites are not responsible for anyone failing any part of any selection process as a result of the information contained within its content, products, website, resources, and videos. How2Become and their authors cannot accept any responsibility for any errors or omissions within these resources, however, caused. No responsibility for loss or damage occasioned by any person acting, or refraining from action, as a result of the material can be accepted by How2Become.

All rights reserved. Apart from any permitted use under UK copyright law no part of this publication may be reproduced or transmitted in any form or by any means, electronic or mechanical, including photocopying, recording, or any information, storage or retrieval system without permission in writing from the publisher or under licence from the Copyright Licensing Agency Limited. Further details of such licenses (for reprographic reproduction) may be obtained from the Copyright Licensing Agency Ltd, Saffron House, 6-10 Kirby Street, London EC1N 8TS.

As part of this product you have also received FREE access to online tests that will help you to pass the Royal Navy selection tests:

To gain access, simply go to:

www.MyPsychometricTests.com

Get more products for passing any test at:

www.How2Become.com

Contents

Introduction ... 7

Preface By Author Richard McMunn ... 11

About The DAA Selection Test ... 13

Tips To Prepare You For The Navy DAA ... 17

Verbal Reasoning Tests ... 21

Numerical Reasoning Tests ... 49

Spatial Reasoning Tests ... 69

Work Rate Tests ... 85

Mechanical Comprehension ... 99

Electrical Comprehension ... 119

A Few Final Words ... 135

Introduction

Welcome to your new guide, *Defence Aptitude Assessment: Sample Test Questions* for the Royal Navy. This guide was written with the rigorous selection process of the Royal Navy in mind.

Here at How2Become, we know how complex the DAA can be. As the UK's leading career and testing specialists, it is our aim to put together a testing guide that will assist you during your preparation.

The selection tests for the Royal Navy are designed to assess potential employees' 'suitability' for specific job posts. When you apply to join the navy as a rating or an officer, you will undergo a challenging selection test, the DAA (more commonly known as the Defence Aptitude Assessment.

With the help of this guide, you will be able to prepare for the types of question you are to face during your Royal Navy selection test. This guide is packed full of testing questions to give you some idea of what you can expect in terms of question type and the skills required.

We have created an easy-to-follow guide that breaks up the selection process into small, manageable sections.

Below we have outlined the contents of this guide:

1. Verbal Reasoning;

2. Numerical Reasoning;

3. Spatial Reasoning;

4. Work Rate;

5. Mechanical Comprehension;

6. Electrical Comprehension;

For best results, we recommend that you work through the guide in the order that it is written. However, if you would like to focus on one particular test, use the contents to locate which test you want to begin.

If you want more information about preparing for life in the Royal Navy, then here at How2Become, we offer a wide range of products to assist you at www.How2Become.com.

Good luck and best wishes,

The How2Become Team

Preface By Author Richard McMunn

Before you get your head into the game, and start practising for your Defence Aptitude Assessment Tests, I thought it might be a good idea to introduce myself; explaining my background, and why I'm qualified to help you pass the selection process for joining the Royal Navy.

At the time of writing, I am 50 years old and living in Tunbridge Wells, Kent. I left school at the usual age of 16 and joined the Royal Navy, serving on-board HMS Invincible as part of 800 Naval Air Squadron which formed part of the Fleet Air Arm. There I was, at the age of 16, travelling the world and working as an engineer on Sea Harrier jets! It was fantastic and I loved every minute of it!

After four years, I left the Royal Navy and joined Kent Fire and Rescue Service as a firefighter. Over the next 17 years, I worked my way up through the ranks to the position of Assistant Divisional Officer. During my time in the fire service, I spent a lot of time working as an instructor at the Fire Brigade Training Centre. I was also involved in the selection process for assessing candidates who wanted to become firefighters. Therefore, my knowledge and experience gained so far in life has been invaluable in helping people like you to pass any type of selection process. I am sure you will find this guide an invaluable resource during your preparation for joining the Royal Navy.

I have always been fortunate in the fact that I persevere in everything I set my mind to. I understand that if I keep working hard in life, then I will always be successful, or at least know that I have done my very best! This is an important lesson that I want you to take on board.

If you work hard and persevere, then success will come your way. The same rule applies when applying for a career in the Armed Forces; if you work hard and make the most out of your preparation time, then you will be successful.

Finally, it is very important that you believe in your own abilities. It does not matter if you have no qualifications; it does not matter if you are currently weak in the area of psychometric testing. What does matter is self-belief, self-discipline, and a genuine desire to improve and become successful.

Best wishes,
Richard McMunn

About The DAA Selection Test

Defence Aptitude Assessment

Before we get into some sample practice questions for the Defence Aptitude Assessment (DAA), let's first recap on what the test actually involves.

The DAA consists of a number of different aptitude tests, which are designed to assess which careers in the Royal Navy you are most suited to. There are many different career opportunities available, and each one requires a different level of skill.

The DAA consists of six timed multiple-choice aptitude tests. These are as follows:

Verbal Reasoning

- This assessment is used to assess candidates' ability to interpret written information.

- In the real assessment, you will be given 15 minutes to answer 20 questions.

Numerical Reasoning

- This assessment is used to assess mathematical knowledge, including arithmetics and data interpretation.

- In the real assessment, the test is split into two sections. In the first section, you will be given 4 minutes to answer 12 questions. In the second section, you will be given 11 minutes to answer 15 questions.

Spatial Reasoning

- This test assesses candidates' ability to work with shapes and 3D objects.

- In the real assessment, you will be given 4 minutes to answer 10 questions for set 1, and 3 minutes for 10 questions in set 2.

Work Rate

- This assessment is an aptitude test which assess candidates' ability to work through routine tasks as quickly and effectively as possible.

- In the real assessment, you will be given 4 minutes to answer 20 questions.

Mechanical Comprehension

- This assessment is an aptitude test which focuses on mechanical concepts.

- In the real assessment, you will be given 10 minutes to answer 20 questions.

Electrical Comprehension

- This assessment is an aptitude test which focuses on electrical concepts.

- In the real assessment, you will be given 11 minutes to answer 21 questions.

Now that you understand what the test will involve, let's move on to some tips. These tips will help you to make the most out of your preparation time.

Read through the tips before attempting the sample tests.

Tips To Prepare You For The Navy DAA

There's no two ways about it, the most effective way in which you can prepare for your assessment, is to carry out lots of sample test questions. When we say lots, we mean lots!

Before we provide you with an array of test questions, here are a few important tips for you to consider:

- It is important that before you sit the DAA , you find out as much information about the nature of the test. Most importantly, you need to find out the type(s) of questions that are going to appear. You should also take steps to find out if the tests will be timed, and also whether or not they will be of a multiple-choice format. By finding out this information prior to your assessment, that means you can tailor your sample tests to mimic the actual nature of the real assessment.

- Variety is the key to success. We recommend that you attempt a variety of different test questions, such as numerical reasoning, verbal reasoning, fault analysis, spatial reasoning and mechanical reasoning. This will undoubtedly improve your overall ability to pass the test. For more help on the aforementioned tests, please check out the following resources on www.How2Become.com.

Tips To Prepare You For The Navy DAA

- Confidence is an important part of preparation. How many times have you sat a test or exam, and your mind goes blank? This happens to the majority of us. This is because you are nervous, stressed and focusing on the negatives. Instead, you need to try to put yourself in a positive mindset. If your confidence is at its peak, then there is no doubt that your test scores will greatly improve.

- Whilst this is a very basic tip that may appear obvious, many people neglect to follow it. Make sure that you get a good nights sleep the night before your DAA. Research has shown that those people who have regular 'good' sleep are far more likely to demonstrate higher concentration levels during psychometric tests.

- Try practising numerical test questions in your head, without writing down your calculations. This is very difficult to accomplish, but it is excellent practice for the real test. Also, practise numerical reasoning tests without a calculator. If you are permitted to use a calculator at the test, make sure you know how to use one!

- You are what you eat! In the week prior to the test, eat and drink healthily. Avoid cigarettes, alcohol and food with high fat content. The reason for this is that these will make you feel sluggish and you will not perform to your best ability on the day. On the morning of your assessment, eat a healthy breakfast such as porridge and a banana.

- ALWAYS drink plenty of water.

- If you have any special needs that need to be catered for, ensure you inform the assessment centre staff PRIOR to the assessment day. By doing so, they will be able to provide you with additional support (such as extra time). This can only work to your advantage, so be sure to let them know of any learning difficulty or other needs.

Now that we have provided you with a number of important tips, take the time to work through the many different sample test questions that are contained within the guide.

In order to complete the tests accurately, use a stopwatch to time yourself for each section.

> **Please note that the tests used in this book are to be used as a GUIDELINE only. Whilst we have tried our best to provide similar tests to the real thing, we cannot guarantee exact exam-style questions.**
>
> **However, these sample tests are a great way to increase the key skills required for each section of the assessment.**

Verbal Reasoning Tests

Defence Aptitude Assessment

During the Defence Aptitude Assessment, you will be required to sit a Verbal Reasoning Test.

Verbal Reasoning is the ability to analyse and comprehend information. The Royal Navy selection process uses this form of aptitude test as a way of measuring candidates' ability to read through information and 'pick out' key information.

Preparing for verbal reasoning assessments can be tricky, but we believe that the best way to prepare, is to have a go at similar verbal reasoning assessments.

During the actual Verbal Reasoning Test with the navy, you will have a specific amount of time to answer each question. Read through each extract carefully and answer the questions that follow.

In the real test, there are 20 questions you need to answer. You will be given 20 minutes to complete this assessment.

VERBAL REASONING PRACTICE QUESTION

> Barry and Bill work at their local supermarket in the town of Whiteham. Barry works every day, except Wednesday. The supermarket is run by Barry's brother, Elliot, who is married to Sarah.
>
> Sarah and Elliot have 2 children, Marcus and Michelle, who are both 7 years old, and they live in the road adjacent to the supermarket.
>
> Barry lives in a town called Redford, which is 7 miles from Whiteham.
>
> Bill's girlfriend Maria works in a factory in her hometown of Brownhaven.
>
> Sarah and Elliot take their children on holiday to Tenford twice a year and Barry usually gives them a lift in his car.
>
> The town of Redford is 6 miles from the seaside town of Tenford.
>
> Barry's mum lives in Tenford and he tries to visit her once a week, at 2pm, when he has a day off work.

Question 1

Which town does Elliot live in?

A. Redford

B. Whiteham

C. Brownhaven

D. Tenford

E. Cannot say

How to answer the question:

When it comes to questions like this, it involves a simple process of elimination.

In the second paragraph, we are told that Sarah and Elliot live adjacent to the supermarket. In the first paragraph, we are told that the supermarket can be located in the town of Whiteham.

Therefore, Elliot must also live in Whiteham.

Question 2

On which day of the week does Barry visit his mother?

A. Cannot say

B. Monday

C. Tuesday

D. Wednesday

E. Thursday

How to answer the question:

Again, it's all about the process of elimination.

In the first paragraph, we are told that Barry works every day except for Wednesdays. In the last paragraph, we are told that Barry visits his mother once a week on a day he is not working.

We know, from reading the first paragraph, that Barry doesn't work Wednesday, so this is the day he would be able to go and visit his mother.

Question 3

Bill and Maria live together in Brownhaven.

A. True

B. False

C. Cannot say

How to answer the question:

From reading the passage, it is not made clear as to whether or not Bill and Maria live together.

Although the passage tells us that Maria works in Brownhaven, it is not made clear as to a) whether she lives there, and b) whether or not Bill lives with her.

Therefore, the answer is C: cannot say.

Now that we've looked at a sample verbal reasoning question, have a go at the following practice test.

VERBAL REASONING EXERCISE 1

Read the following information carefully before answering the questions that follow. You have 5 minutes to complete exercise 1.

> **FLAT A** is located in a town. It is 12 miles from the nearest train station. It has 2 bedrooms and is located on the ground floor. The monthly rental is £450 and the council tax is £50 per month. The lease is for 6 months.
>
> **FLAT B** is located in the city centre and is 2 miles from the nearest train station. It is located on the 3rd floor. The monthly rental is £600 and the council tax is £130 per month. The lease is for 6 months and it has 3 bedrooms.
>
> **FLAT C** is located in the city centre and is 3 miles from the nearest train station. It is located on the 1st floor and has 1 bedroom. The monthly rental is £550 and the council tax is £100 per month. The lease is for 12 months.
>
> **FLAT D** is located in a town. The monthly rental is £395 per month and the council tax is £100 per month. It is located on the ground floor and the lease is for 6 months. It is 18 miles from the nearest train station. The flat has 2 bedrooms.
>
> **FLAT E** is located in a village and is 12 miles from the nearest train station. It has 3 bedrooms and is located on the 2nd floor. The monthly rental is £375 and the council tax is £62. It has a lease of 12 months.

Question 1. You want a flat that is within 10 miles of the nearest train station, and is located on the 1st floor or lower. The combined monthly rent and council tax bill must be no greater than £600. Which flat would you choose?

A. Flat A

B. Flat B

C. Flat C

D. Flat D

E. None of the above

Question 2. You want a flat that has at least 2 bedrooms and has a combined monthly rent and tax bill that does not exceed £450. Which flat would you choose?

A. Flat A

B. Flat B

C. Flat C

D. Flat D

E. Flat E

Question 3. You want a flat that has a combined monthly rent and council tax bill that is not in excess to £700. It needs to be within 15 miles of the train station, and have a lease for 6 months. Which flat would you choose?

A. Flat A

B. Flat B

C. Flat C

D. Flat D

E. Flat E

VERBAL REASONING EXERCISE 2

Read the following information carefully before answering the questions that follow.

You have 5 minutes to complete exercise 2.

> Cardiovascular disease is so prevalent that virtually all businesses are likely to have employees who suffer from, or may develop, this condition.
>
> Research shows that between 51-80% of all people who suffer a heart attack, are able to return to work. However, this may not be possible if they have previously been involved in heavy physical work.
>
> In such cases, it may be possible to move the employee to lighter duties, with appropriate retraining where necessary.
>
> Similarly, high-pressure, stressful work, even where it does not involve physical activity, should also be avoided.
>
> Human Resources managers should be aware of the implications of job roles for employees with a cardiac condition.

Question 1. Physical or stressful work may bring on a heart attack.

A. True

B. False

C. Cannot say

Question 2. The majority of people who have suffered a heart attack can later return to work.

A. True

B. False

C. Cannot say

Question 3. Heart disease may affect employees in any type of business.

A. True

B. False

C. Cannot say

Defence Aptitude Assessment

VERBAL REASONING EXERCISE 3

Read the following information carefully before answering the questions that follow.

You have 5 minutes to complete exercise 3.

Although there is not a clear cause for abdominal pain in children, it may be a symptom of emotional disturbance, especially where it appears in conjunction with phobias or sleep disorders such as nightmares or sleep-walking.

It may also be linked to eating habits: a study carried out in the USA found that children with pain tended to be fussier about what and how much they ate, and to have over-anxious parents who spent a considerable amount of time trying to persuade them to eat.

Although abdominal pain had previously been linked to excessive milk-drinking, this research found that children with pain drank rather less milk than those in the control group.

Question 1. There is no clear cause for abdominal pain in children.

A. True

B. False

C. Cannot say

Question 2. Abdominal pain in children is caused by eating too much.

A. True

B. False

C. Cannot say

Question 3. Drinking milk may help to prevent abdominal pain in children.

A. True

B. False

C. Cannot say

VERBAL REASONING EXERCISE 4

Read the following information carefully before answering the questions that follow.

You have 5 minutes to complete exercise 4.

> Jeff Roberts claims he has had his garden shed broken into. A crowbar was found in the garden and the door of the shed had been forced open. Mr Roberts claims that a lawn mower, a strimmer, a new spade and a garden fork have been stolen.
>
> He says that last week a group of young people graffitied the side wall of his house and he thinks they are to blame.
>
> The ringleader of the gang, Sam Smith, has recently started a gardening company.
>
> The latest reported facts are:
>
> - Sam Smith has previous convictions for breaking and entering.
>
> - Sam Smith has a variety of new gardening equipment for his company – including a spade the same as Mr Roberts.
>
> - Mr Roberts' spade was bought from popular high street shop.
>
> - Mr Roberts stolen items are worth £400.
>
> - Mr Roberts says Sam Smith has been harassing him.
>
> - Sam Smith's dad fired Mr Roberts from his marketing company last month.

Question 1. Mr Roberts has a grudge against Sam Smith.

A. True

B. False

C. Cannot say

Question 2. The items stolen from Mr Roberts' shed are worth more than £400.

A. True

B. False

C. Cannot say

Question 3. Sam Smith may have stolen Mr Roberts' spade.

A. True

B. False

C. Cannot say

VERBAL REASONING EXERCISE 5

Read the following information carefully before answering the questions that follow.

You have 5 minutes to complete exercise 5.

> Below is a company ordering process.
>
> 1.1 Our display of products and online services on our website are an invitation and not an offer to sell those goods to you.
>
> 1.2 An offer is made when you place the order for your products or online service. However, we will not have made a contract with you unless and until we accept your offer.
>
> 1.3 We take payment from your card when we process your order and have checked your card details. Goods are subject to availability. If we are unable to supply the goods, we will inform you of this as soon as possible. A full refund will be given if you have already paid for the goods. It is our aim to always keep our website updated and all goods displayed are available.
>
> 1.4 If you enter a correct email address, we will send you an order acknowledgement email immediately, along with a receipt of payment. These do not constitute an order confirmation or order acceptance from us.
>
> 1.5 Unless we have notified you that we do not accept your order or you have cancelled it, order acceptance and the creation of the contract between you and us will take place at the point the goods have ordered are dispatched from our premises.
>
> 1.6 The contract will be formed at the place of dispatch of the goods. All goods, wherever possible, will be dispatched within 24 hours of the order being placed, Monday to Thursday. If your order falls on a weekend or bank holiday, your order will be dispatched on the next available working day. All orders are sent recorded delivery, and will require a signature. In the majority of cases, however, we will dispatch goods using Royal Mail's standard First Class delivery service.

Question 1. If a customer places an order, and they have entered a correct email address, they will immediately receive an order confirmation email.

A. True

B. False

C. Cannot say

Question 2. Orders placed on a Friday will be dispatched on a Saturday.

A. True

B. False

C. Cannot say

Question 3. Payment is taken from the card once the card details have been checked.

A. True

B. False

C. Cannot say

VERBAL REASONING EXERCISE 6

Read the following information carefully before answering the questions that follow.

You have 5 minutes to complete exercise 6.

> The Special Air Service was originally founded by Lieutenant David Stirling during World War II. The initial purpose of the regiment was to be a long-range desert patrol group required to conduct raids and sabotage operations far behind the enemy lines.
>
> Lieutenant Stirling was a member of Number 8 Commando Regiment and he specifically looked for recruits who were both talented and individual specialists in their field. He looked for initiative.
>
> The first mission of the SAS turned out to be a disaster. They were operating in support of Field Marshal Calude Auchinleck's attack in November 1941, but only 22 out of 62 SAS troopers deployed reached the rendezvous point. However, Stirling still managed to organise another attack against the German airfields at Aqedabia, Site of Agheila, which successfully destroyed 61 enemy aircraft, without a single casualty. After that, the 1st SAS earned regimental status and Stirling's brother, Bill, began to arrange a second regiment called Number 2 SAS.
>
> It was during the desert war that they performed a number of successful insertion missions and destroyed many aircraft and fuel depots in the process. Their success contributed towards Hitler issuing his Kommandobefehl order to execute all captured Commandos. The Germans then stepped up security and as a result, the SAS changed their tactics. They used jeeps armed with Vickers K machine guns and used tracer ammunition to ignite fuel and aircraft. When the Italians captured David Stirling, he was sent to Colditz Castle and was held as a prisoner of war for the remainder of World War II. His brother, Bill, and 'Paddy' Blair Mayne, then took command of the regiment.

Question 1. During the SAS's first mission, only 42 of the total troopers deployed reached the rendezvous point.

A. True

B. False

C. Cannot say

Question 2. When the Germans captured David Stirling, he ended up in Colditz Castle as a prisoner for the remainder of the war.

A. True

B. False

C. Cannot say

Question 3. Lieutenant Stirling was member of Number 8 SAS Regiment.

A. True

B. False

C. Cannot say

VERBAL REASONING EXERCISE 7

Read the following information carefully before answering the questions that follow.

You have 5 minutes to complete exercise 7.

> Brendon and his youngest brother, Jason, live in the middle of Maidstone. It is a short walking distance from their house to the supermarket. Every morning, they walk the same route and part at the supermarket, which is where Brendon works. Jason continues his journey with his friend, Pete. Every morning, they make their way to Linton College, a 2-minute walk from the supermarket.
>
> Madeline lives in a small village on the outskirts of the town where she used to live. Her sister, Rachel, attends a grammar school in Tunbridge Wells. She travels from her house in Marden via train, to get to school each day. Most days, Rachel sits next to her friend Matt on the train.
>
> Matt gets on the train in his home town of Staplehurst. When Matt doesn't get the train, he drives his sister's car. His sister is called Polly and she too, works at the same supermarket as Brendon.

Question 1. Where does Polly work?

A. Staplehurst

B. Marden

C. Maidstone

D. Tunbridge Wells

Question 2. Where does Rachel go to school?

A. Staplehurst

B. Marden

C. Maidstone

D. Tunbridge Wells

Question 3. Which of the following is definitely true?

A. Brendon is older than Jason.

B. Jason is older than Pete.

C. Brendon is older than Polly.

D. Madeline is older than Rachel.

VERBAL REASONING EXERCISE 8

Read the following information carefully before answering the questions that follow.

You have 5 minutes to complete exercise 8.

Under the Race Relations (Amendment) Act, public authorities (including the Fire and Rescue Service) have a general duty to promote race equality. This means that when carrying out their functions or duties, they must have due regard to the need to:

- Eliminate discrimination;

- Promote equality of opportunity;

- Promote good relations between persons of different racial groups.

In order to demonstrate how Fire and Rescue Service plan to meet their statutory duties, they have an obligation to produce and publish what is called a Race Equality Scheme. The Race Equality Scheme outlines their strategy and action plan to ensure that equality and diversity are mainstreamed through their policies, practices, procedures and functions. Central to this strategy are external consultation, monitoring and assessment, training, and ensuring that the public have access to this information.

"Equality is not about treating everybody the same, but recognising we are all individuals, unique in our own way. Equality and fairness is about recognising, accepting and valuing people's unique individuality according to their needs. This often means that individuals may be treated appropriately, yet fairly, based on their needs."

Verbal Reasoning Tests

Question 1. Any form of racism is unwelcome in the Fire Service.

A. True

B. False

C. Cannot say

Question 2. The general public does have access to the Race Equality Scheme.

A. True

B. False

C. Cannot say

Question 3. The Fire Service may promote good relations between persons of different racial groups.

A. True

B. False

C. Cannot say

VERBAL REASONING EXERCISE 9

Read the following information carefully before answering the questions that follow.

You have 5 minutes to complete exercise 9.

> The summers in Australia can bring total devastation to many through the many bushfires which occur. Bushfires destroy livelihoods, property, machinery, eucalyptus forests and they can even spread to the suburban areas of major cities.
>
> Although all bushfires can have a devastating effect, few of them fall under the 'disaster' category. Some of these falling into this category are:
>
> - Victoria (2009): 173 lives were lost in this bushfire, so it is more commonly referred to as Black Saturday;
> - South Australia and Victoria (1983): This claimed 76 lives and was named as Ash Wednesday;
> - Southern Victoria (1969): 23 lives were claimed;
> - New South Wales (1968): There were 14 fatalities in this bushfire in the Blue Mountains and coastal region;
> - Hobart and Southern Tasmania (1967): 62 people were killed;
> - Victoria (1939): This was named Black Friday after 71 people lost their lives.
>
> There are two different types of bushfire in Australia – grass fires and forest fires. Grass fires more commonly occur on grazing and farm land. These often destroy fences, livestock, machinery, and sometimes human lives. Forest fires are largely made up of eucalyptus trees. These are extremely difficult to control due to the high amounts of flammable vapour from the leaves. The bushfires are fought by large numbers of trained volunteer firefighters. Helicopters and light aircraft are sometimes used to make observations about the fire and some also have the capacity to carry water. Aircraft used to carry water in order to extinguish forest fires often find that the visibility is extremely poor, preventing them from getting close enough to the fire in order to extinguish it with their quantities of water.

Question 1. Aircraft deployed to extinguish bushfires struggle to get close to the fire due to the heat.

A. True

B. False

C. Cannot say

Question 2. In total, there have been 419 fatalities from Australian bushfires since 1939.

A. True

B. False

C. Cannot say

Question 3. Hundreds of animals are killed by bushfires each year.

A. True

B. False

C. Cannot say

VERBAL REASONING EXERCISE 10

Read the following information carefully before answering the questions that follow.

You have 5 minutes to complete exercise 10.

> There are two separate options offered for account billing:
>
> Monthly: This option operates on a 4-week cycle beginning on the day of account activation.
> Annually: This option operates on a 365-day cycle beginning on the day of account activation.
>
> Note: Customers on a monthly billing cycle are billed every 4 weeks.
>
> When your account reaches its appropriate billing day (your account's expiration date), your credit card will be automatically billed for the next billing cycle and your account expiration date will be extended by an additional 4 weeks (or 365 for annual packages). You will receive a receipt via email. If the transaction is unsuccessful for any reason, we will attempt to re-bill your credit card for 2 consecutive days and send an unsuccessful renewal email for each unsuccessful attempt (to your accounts specified Billing Profile email address).
>
> After your first unsuccessful renewal attempt, your account status will be updated to Billing Hold Level 1. This status indicates that your account is overdue but otherwise has no direct effect on your service which will continue for up to 4 weeks following your actual expiration date.
>
> 4 weeks after your account expires, we will attempt to re-bill your credit card for two monthly payments. If successful, your account expiration date will be extended by an additional 4 weeks (from bill date) and you will receive a receipt via email. If unsuccessful, your account status will be updated to Billing Hold Level 2. This status indicates that your account is now more than 4 weeks overdue and will close all account service until payment has been received. We will attempt to re-bill your credit card for 2 consecutive days and send an unsuccessful renewal email for each unsuccessful attempt.
>
> When your account is in this status, you will still be able to log in and access both the Earn Cash page (to manage affiliate referrals and the Renew Account page).

> 56 days after your account expires, we will attempt to re-bill your credit card for three monthly payments. If successful, your account expiration date will be extended by an additional 3 weeks (from bill date), your account will be reactivated and you will receive a receipt via email. If unsuccessful, your account will be permanently closed.

Question 1. Billing Hold Level 1 occurs after the first unsuccessful renewal attempt.

A. True

B. False

C. Cannot say

Question 2. Billing Hold Level 2 occurs when an attempt to take two monthly payments after an account is 4 weeks past account expiration fails.

A. True

B. False

C. Cannot say

Question 3. Customers who opt for the monthly billing option will be billed every 4 weeks on the first day of each month.

A. True

B. False

C. Cannot say

ANSWERS TO VERBAL REASONING TESTS

EXERCISE 1

1. E

2. E

3. A

EXERCISE 2

1. C

2. A

3. A

EXERCISE 3

1. A

2. C

3. C

EXERCISE 4

1. C

2. C

3. A

EXERCISE 5

1. B

2. B

3. A

EXERCISE 6

1. B

2. B

3. B

EXERCISE 7

1. C

2. D

3. A

EXERCISE 8

1. A

2. A

3. B

EXERCISE 9

1. B

2. C

3. C

EXERCISE 10

1. A

2. A

3. C

Numerical Reasoning Tests

Defence Aptitude Assessment

During the Defence Aptitude Assessment, you will be required to undertake a Numerical Reasoning Test. This test is used to determine how accurately you can interpret numerical information such as charts, graphs and tables. These will also assess your ability to use fractions, decimals and other basic arithmetic.

As you can imagine, the most effective way to prepare for this type of test is to carry out lots of sample numerical reasoning test questions, without the aid of a calculator!

In the real test, you will have 4 minutes to complete 12 questions in part 1, and 11 minutes to complete 15 questions for part 2.

Before we begin, let's quickly take a look at some of the mathematical topics that you should revise BEFORE sitting your numerical assessment.

Fractions	Decimals	Percentages
Values	Basic Arithmetic	Basic Algebra
Charts	Tables	Graphs

Numerical Reasoning Tests

NUMERICAL REASONING EXERCISE 1

You have 10 minutes to complete the 20 questions.

Question 1. Your friends tell you that their electricity bill has gone up from £40 per month to £47 per month. By what percentage has their bill increased for the year?

A	B	C	D	E
18%	16.5%	22%	17.5%	15%

Question 2. A woman earns a salary of £32,000 per year. How much would she earn in 15 years if she receives a 5% salary increase every 5 years?

A	B	C	D	E
£504,000	£380,600	£504,400	£460,200	£480,000

Question 3. Rachel works out that her flight will travel at a speed of 1,200km/h for 3.5 hours in order to arrive at her destination. If the flight was to cover the same distance but in a time of 1 hour and 30 minutes, the plane must travel at what speed (km/h)?

A	B	C	D	E
600 km/h	1,750 mm/h	1,800 km/h	2,600 km/h	2,800 km/h

Question 4. What is the value of x?

$$\frac{6x - 4}{2} = 19$$

A	B	C	D	E
5	7	9	11	13

Question 5. Ellie spends 3 hours on the phone talking to her friend abroad. If the call costs 12 pence per 5 minutes, how much does the call cost?

A	B	C	D	E
£3.30	£4.32	£3.32	£4.44	£3.44

Question 6. A woman spends £27 in a retail store. She has a discount voucher that reduces the total cost from £27 to £21.60. What percentage was her discount voucher worth?

A	B	C	D	E
5%	10%	15%	20%	25%

Question 7. A group of 7 men spend £21.70 on a round of drinks. If the bill was split equally, how much would each person pay?

A	B	C	D	E
£3.00	£6.10	£3.10	£3.15	£3.20

Question 8. 45,600 people attend a football match to watch Manchester United play Tottenham Hotspur. If there are 32,705 Manchester United supporters at the game, what fraction of the attendees are Tottenham Hotspur supporters? Give your answer in it's simplest form.

A	B	C	D	E
$16/23$	$2579/9120$	$613/780$	$147/780$	$6541/9120$

Question 9. Calculate $5/7 - 2/3$

A	B	C	D	E
$2/3$	$1/21$	$1/11$	$3/21$	$3/4$

Numerical Reasoning Tests

Question 10. A car journey usually takes 6 hours and 55 minutes, but on one occasion the car stops for a total of 47 minutes. How long does the journey take on this occasion?

A	B	C	D	E
6 hours and 40 minutes	5 hours and 45 minutes	7 hours and 40 minutes	7 hours and 42 minutes	6 hours and 42 minutes

Question 11. There are 10 people in a team. Five of them weigh 70 kg each, and the remaining five weigh 75 kg each. Work out the average weight of the team.

A	B	C	D	E
72.5 kg	71.5 kg	70.5 kg	72 kg	71 kg

Question 12. Calculate 3.83 + 8.43

A	B	C	D	E
13.13	12.61	13.31	12.26	11.12

Question 13. What is ⅗ as a decimal?

A	B	C	D	E
0.60	0.30	0.25	0.40	0.35

Question 14. Using the rule of BIDMAS, work out 23.7 − 2.5 × 8.

A	B	C	D	E
169.6	3.7	4.8	196.6	130.6

Defence Aptitude Assessment

Question 15. How many grams are there in 2.5 kilograms?

A	B	C	D	E
0.0025 g	250 g	2005 g	2,500 g	0.25 g

Question 16. Work out

$$\frac{4}{6} \times \frac{3}{5}$$

A	B	C	D	E
12/25	12/40	6/20	2/5	1/5

Question 17. What is one quarter of 6 hours?

A	B	C	D	E
30 minutes	15 minutes	1 hour	1 hour and 30 minutes	2 hours and 15 minutes

Question 18. When paying a bill at the bank, you give the cashier one £20 note, two £5 notes, seven £1 coins, twelve 10p coins, and seventeen 2p coins. How much have you given the cashier?

A	B	C	D	E
£38.54	£43.46	£34.46	£63.44	£36.36

Question 19. If there are 610 metres in a mile, how many metres are there in 4 miles − 50 metres + 2 miles + 15 metres − 1 mile?

A	B	C	D	E
3,870 metres	3,955 metres	3,510 metres	3,205 metres	3,015 metres

Question 20. A worker is required to work for 8 hours a day. He is entitled to three 20-minute breaks, and an hour for lunch during the working day. If he works for 5 days per week for 4 weeks, how many hours will he have actually worked?

A	B	C	D	E
12 hours	14 hours	120 hours	140 hours	150 hours

NUMERICAL REASONING EXERCISE 1 ANSWERS

Q1. D = 17.5%

£40 × 12 = £480
£47 × 12 = £564
(564 − 480) ÷ 480 = 0.175
0.175 × 100 = 17.5

Q2. C = £504,400

£32,000 × 5 = £160,000
£32,000 × 1.05 = £33,600
£33,600 × 5 = £168,000
£33,600 × 1.05 = £35,280
£35,280 × 5 = £176,400
£160,000 + £168,000 + £176,400 = £504,400

Q3. E = 2,800km/h

1,200 × 3.5 = 4,200
4,200 ÷ 1.5 = 2,800

Q4. B = 7

$$\frac{6x - 4}{2} = 19$$

Multiply both sides by 2: $6x - 4 = 38$
Subtract 4 from both sides: $6x = 42$
Divide both sides by 6: $x = 7$

Q5. B = £4.32

3 × 60 = 180 minutes
180 minutes ÷ 5 = 36
36 × 12p = £4.32

Numerical Reasoning Tests

Q6. D = 20%

£27 − £21.60 = £5.40
5.4 ÷ £27 = 0.2
0.2 × 100 = 20

Q7. C = £3.10

£21.70 ÷ 7 = £3.10

Q8. B = $^{2579}/_{9120}$

45,600 − 32,705 = 12,895
12,895 and 45,600 are both divisible by 5
12,895 ÷ 5 = 2,579
45,600 ÷ 5 = 9,120

Q9. B = $1/21$

$$\frac{5}{7} - \frac{2}{3} = \frac{15}{21} - \frac{14}{21} = \frac{1}{21}$$

Q10. D = 7 hrs 42 minutes

6 hrs and 55 minutes + 47 minutes = 7 hrs and 42 minutes.

Q11. A = 72.5 kg

(5 × 70) + (5 × 75) = 725 kg.
725 ÷ 10 = 72.5 kg

Q12. D = 12.26

3.83 + 8.43 = 12.26

Q13. A = 0.60

3 ÷ 5 = 0.6

OR

$$\frac{3}{5} = \frac{6}{10}$$

$$\frac{6}{10} = 0.6$$

Q14. B = 3.7

This question asks you to use the method of BIDMAS:
2.5 × 8 = 20
23.7 − 20 = 3.7

Q15. D = 2,500g

There are 1,000g in 1 kilogram. Therefore, 2,500g is equivalent to 2.5 kg (2.5 × 1,000 = 2,500g).

Q16. D = 2/5

4 × 3 = 12
5 × 6 = 30. So, 12/30 in its simplest form = 2/5

Q16. D = 2/5

$$\frac{4}{6} \times \frac{3}{5} = \frac{12}{30} = \frac{2}{5}$$

Q17. D = 1 hour and 30 minutes

6 (hours) × 60 (minutes) = 360 minutes. So, 360 (minutes) ÷ 4 (1/4) = 90 minutes.

Q18. A = £38.54

£20 + £10 + £7 + £1.20 + £0.34 = £38.54

Q19. E = 3,015 metres

2,440 − 50 + 1,220 + 15 − 610 = 3,015

Q20. C = 120 hours

8 hours − 1 hour break − 3 × 20 minutes = 6 hours
6 hours × 5 days = 30 hours
30 hours × 4 weeks = 120 hours

Numerical Reasoning Tests

NUMERICAL REASONING EXERCISE 2

You have 20 minutes to complete the 15 questions.

Question 1. The following table shows the prices to place different sized advertisements in the main section of a newspaper.

ADVERTISEMENT PRICES		
Size of the Advertisement	Colour	Mono
24 x 10	£12,435	£8,567
22 x 5	£6,437	£4,218
8 x 10	£4,208	£3,987
7 x 5	£2,576	£1,340

How much more does it cost a company to place two 24 × 10 mono advertisements and one 22 × 5 colour advertisement, compared to a company placing three 8 × 10 colour advertisements and one 7 × 5 mono advertisement?

A	B	C	D	E
£5,040	£1,365	£10,460	£9,607	£2,464

Question 2. Below is a table of the total staff at Company A (Staff Distribution).

	HR (%)	Sales (%)	Finance (%)	Media (%)	Distribution (%)	TOTAL (%)
Year 1	21	8	19	32	20	100
Year 2	28	11	17	28	16	100
Year 3	16	21	19	25	18	100
Year 4	13	30	21	11	22	100
Year 5	4	9	25	33	24	100
Year 6	20	27	25	12	16	100

In Year 4, there were 504 people employed in Finance. How many people in total were employed in Year 4 in the department of Sales?

A	B	C	D	E
650	550	840	720	880

Question 3. Below is a pie-chart representing crime in the town of Upton. Based on an estimated 200 crimes, use the pie-chart below to estimate the number of burglary-related crimes.

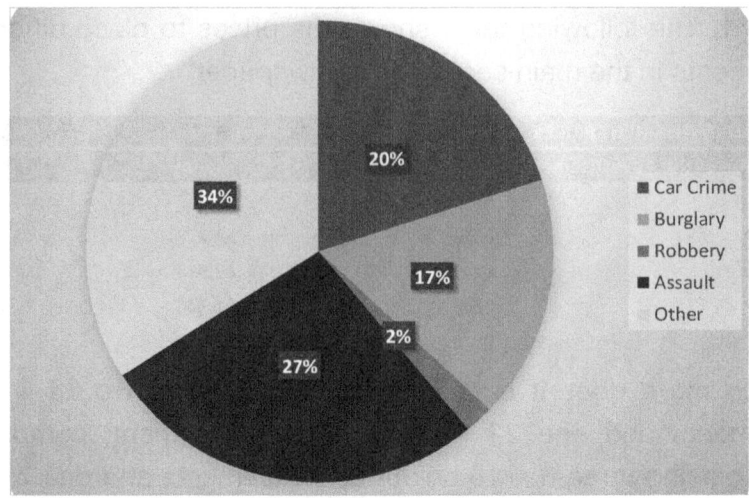

A	B	C	D	E
34	17	27	38	170

Question 4. If I were leaving from Hammersmith, what train time is best to catch if I wish to arrive in Franks Park just before 9 o'clock?

	Train 1	Train 2	Train 3	Train 4
Petersberg	6.45	7.04	------	8.04
Hammersmith	7.00	------	7.45	8.19
St Leonard's Station	7.12	7.20	8.00	------
Mariweather	7.36	7.42	------	8.30
Goldsberg	7.52	------	8.19	8.48
Upperside	8.12	8.04	8.27	9.04
Franks Park	8.30	8.27	8.48	9.28

A	B	C	D	E
7.04	8.04	7.45	7.00	8.19

Question 5. Below is a table listing the percentage changes from 2014 to 2016 for five different companies.

COMPANY	Percentage Change from 2014-2015	Percentage Change from 2015-2016
Company A	+17%	-5%
Company B	+12%	+5%
Company C	-11%	+8%
Company D	-5%	-7%
Company E	+8%	-3%

Using the above table, if company B earned £412,500 in 2014, how much money did the company make in 2016?

A	B	C	D	E
£316,975	£462,000	£415,290	£485,100	£420,000

Question 6. In a survey, people had to choose either A, B, C or D.

The percentages for A, C and D are shown below.

A	B	C	D
25%		30%	15%

320 people chose A. How many people chose option B?

A	B	C	D	E
215	384	429	502	301

The following sign shows the opening times for a zoo.

Zoo Opening Times

March - June	Daily	9:00am to 5:30pm
July - August	Daily	9:00am to 8:00pm
September - February	Saturday and Sunday	10:00am to 4:00pm

Last admission is <u>2 hours</u> before the zoo closes.

Question 7. How many months of the year is the zoo closed on weekdays?

A	B	C	D	E
4	5	6	3	2

Question 8. Kelly goes to the zoo in July. She arrives at 2pm. How many hours can she spend there until it closes?

A	B	C	D	E
3 hours	1 hour	6 hours	5 hours	4 hours

Question 9. Marcus has a season ticket for 2017, allowing him multiple visits at a reduced price. He visits the zoo the following times throughout the year:

Once in January, arriving when the park opens and leaving 2 hours before last admission.
Once in May, arriving at 3:00pm and leaving an hour before closing time.
Once in July, arriving one hour after the park opens and leaving 5 hours before closing time.
Once in August, arriving at 4pm and staying until closing time.

How much time did Marcus spend in the zoo in 2017 in hours and minutes?

A	B	C	D	E
12 hours	12 hours and 30 minutes	10 hours	11 hours and 30 minutes	14 hours

Question 10. The graph shows respondents' answers when asked what their most frequent form of technological communication was.

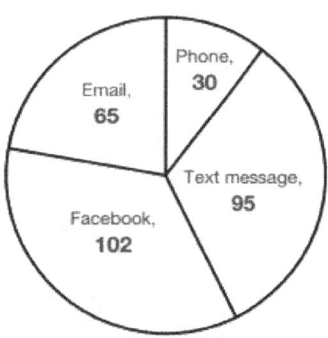

Among the respondents, 75% of all respondents said that it was easier to get in touch with someone through technological communications based on convenience.

How many people said that it was easier to use technological communications based on convenience?

A	B	C	D	E
212	119	227	219	176

Question 11. Below shows a velocity-time graph which a student has drawn to represent the acceleration of an object.

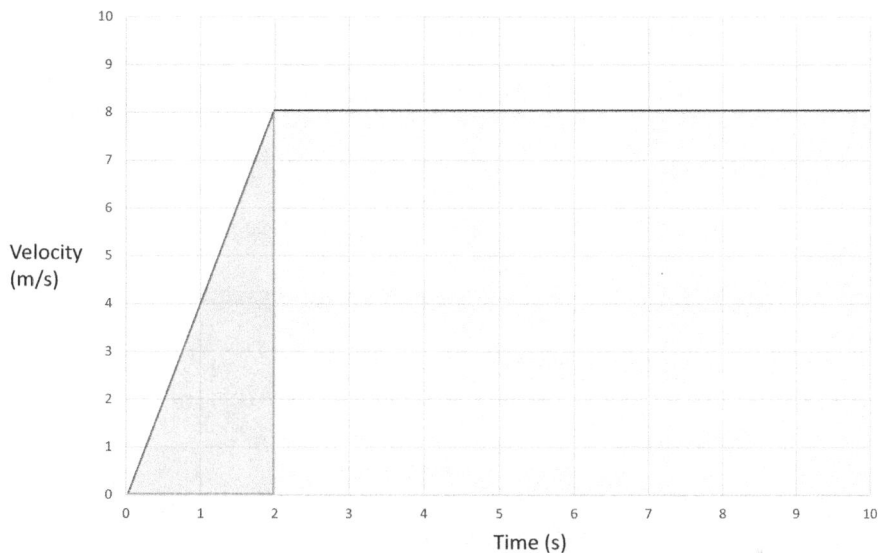

Assuming the object continues to maintain its acceleration at the same rate of speed, how many seconds will it take the object to have a velocity of 64?

A	B	C	D	E
12 seconds	13 seconds	14 seconds	15 seconds	16 seconds

Question 12. See below a table of values representing the formula $9(x + 5)$. Some of the boxes have already been filled in. Using the values already in the table, fill in the missing gaps.

x	$9(x + 5)$
10	135
	81
6	

Question 13. The bar chart below shows the number of people who applied for a Sales Assistant job. The job was advertised for one week, and the bars on the chart represent each day of the week up until the closing date.

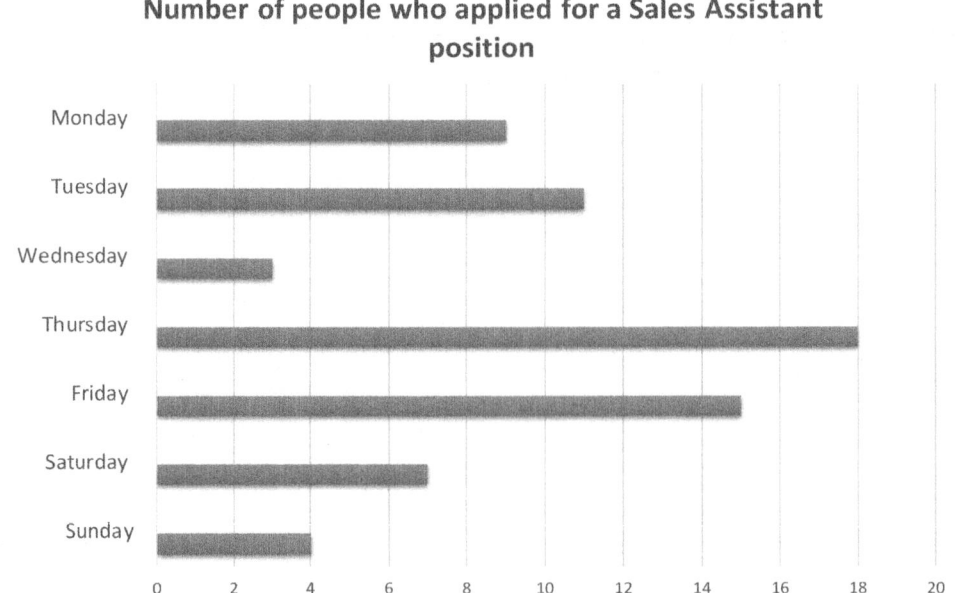

On Wednesday, 3 people applied for the job.

Work out how many people applied for the Sales Assistant position overall.

A	B	C	D	E
58	59	63	67	72

Question 14. The table shows the total tax paid in $ on annual taxable income. For example, a person with an annual taxable income of $60,000 will pay $4,990 plus 25% of ($60,000 - $36,250).

Annual Taxable Income Bracket ($)	Tax Rate	Total Tax paid at the top of this bracket ($)
0-8,950	10%	895
8,950-36,250	15%	4,990
36,250-87,850	25%	17,890
87,850-183,250	28%	44,602
183,250-400,000	33%	116,129.50
Over 400,000	39.6%	

Sam has an annual taxable income of $18,500. How much income tax does he have to pay, to the nearest $?

A	B	C	D	E
$2,328	$2,456	$2,139	$1,985	$3,457

Question 15. A traveller visits three cities, driving in a triangular route.

Start	Finish	Distance	Time Taken
City A	City B	25 km	60 minutes
City B	City C	20 km	30 minutes
City C	City A	75 km	90 minutes

Calculate the traveller's average speed.

A	B	C	D	E
40 km/h	35 km/h	70 km/h	65 km/h	55 km/h

Defence Aptitude Assessment

NUMERICAL REASONING EXERCISE 2 ANSWERS

Q1. D = £9,607

(2 × £8,567) + (1 × £6,437) = £23,571
(3 × £4,208) + (1 × £1,340) = £13,964
£23,571 − £13.964 = £9,607

Q2. D = 720

504 ÷ 0.21 = 2,400
2,400 ÷ 100 × 30 = 720

Q3. A = 34

200 ÷ 100 × 17 = 34

Q4. C = 7.45

If you were leaving from Hammersmith, that means you need to focus on the second row of train times (don't count the train times from Petersberg). You want to arrive in Franks Park just before 9 o'clock, so you would need to catch the 7.45 train from Hammersmith.

Q5. D = £485,100

£412,500 × 1.12 = £462,000
£462,000 × 1.05 = £485,100

Q6. B = 384

320 × 4 = 1,280
100% − (25% + 30% + 15%) = 30%
1,280 × 0.3 = 384

Q7. C = 6 months

September, October, November, December, January and February.

Q8. C = 6 hours

2pm until 8pm

Q9. B = 12 hours and 30 minutes

10:00am til 12 noon = 2 hours
3:00pm til 4:30pm = 1 hour 30 minutes

10:00am til 3:00pm = 5 hours
4:00pm til 8:00pm = 4 hours
2 + 1.5 + 5 + 4 = 12.5 (12 hours and 30 minutes)

Q10. D = 219

65 + 30 + 95 + 102 = 292
292 × 0.75 = 219

Q11. E = 16 seconds

1 second per 4 m/s.
64 ÷ 4 = 16 seconds

Q12.

x	$9(x + 5)$
10	135
4	81
6	**99**

81 ÷ 9 = 9   6 + 5 = 11
9 − 5 = 4   11 × 9 = 99

Q13. D = 67

9 + 11 + 3 + 18 + 15 + 7 + 4 = 67

Q14. A = $2,328

$895 + ($9,550 × 0.15) = $2,327.50

Q15. A = 40 km/h

(25 km + 20 km + 75 km) ÷ (1 + 0.5 + 1.5) = 40

Spatial Reasoning Tests

Defence Aptitude Assessment

During the Defence Aptitude Assessment, you will be required to undertake a Spatial Reasoning Test.

The definition of spatial reasoning is as follows:

> "The ability to interpret and make drawings from mental images and visualise movement or change in those images."

During the DAA, you will be confronted with a number of spatial reasoning questions, and the only effective way to prepare for them is to try as many sample questions as you can.

In the real test, you will be given 4 minutes to answer 10 questions for part 1. For part 2, you will be given 3 minutes to answer 10 questions.

SPATIAL REASONING PRACTICE QUESTION 1

Take a look at the following three shapes. Note the letters on the side of each shape.

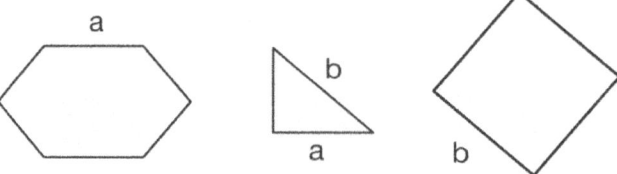

Your task is to join all three shapes together using the corresponding letters. This would make the following shape:

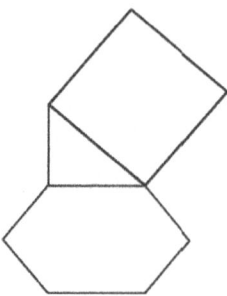

Spatial Reasoning Tests

SPATIAL REASONING EXERCISE 1

You have 4 minutes to complete the 10 questions.

Question 1

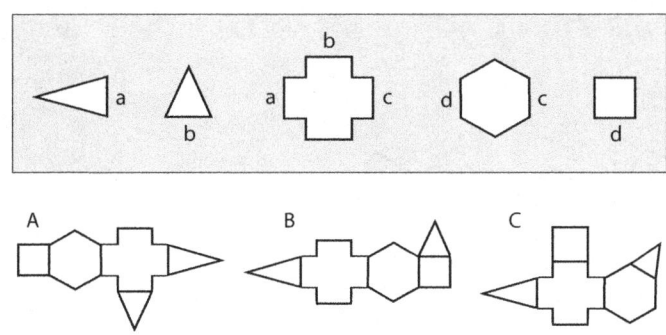

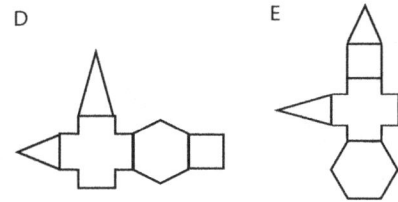

Question 2

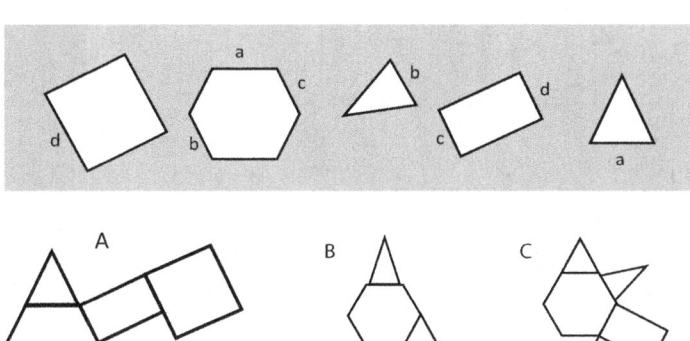

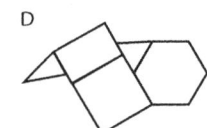

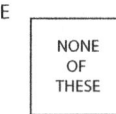

NONE OF THESE

Question 3

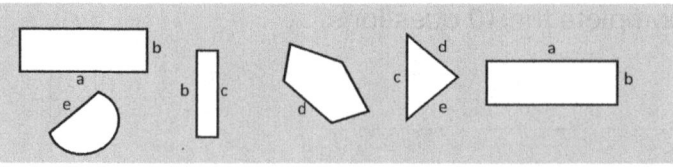

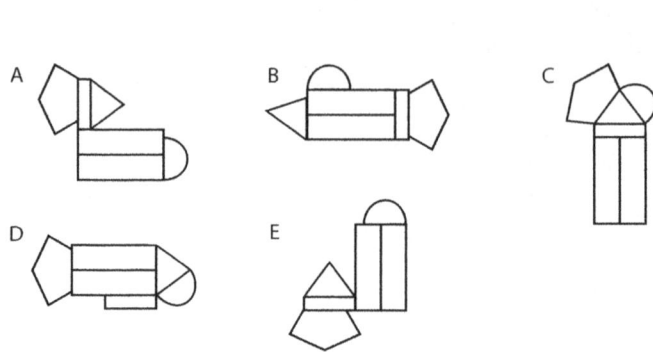

Question 4

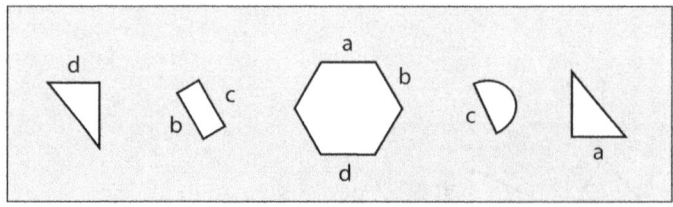

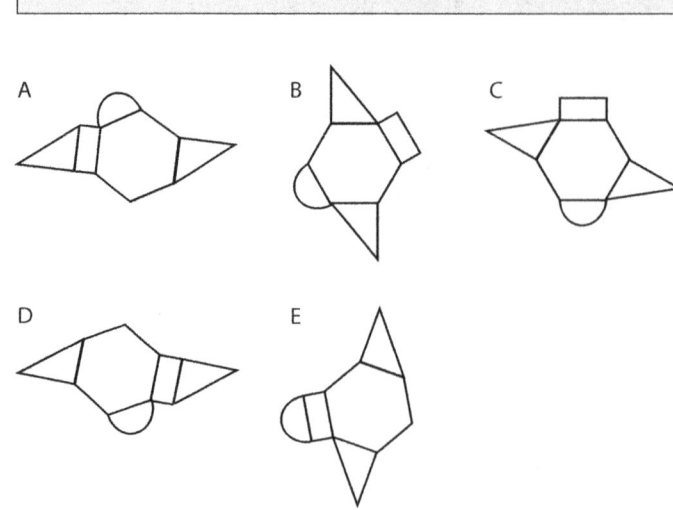

Question 5

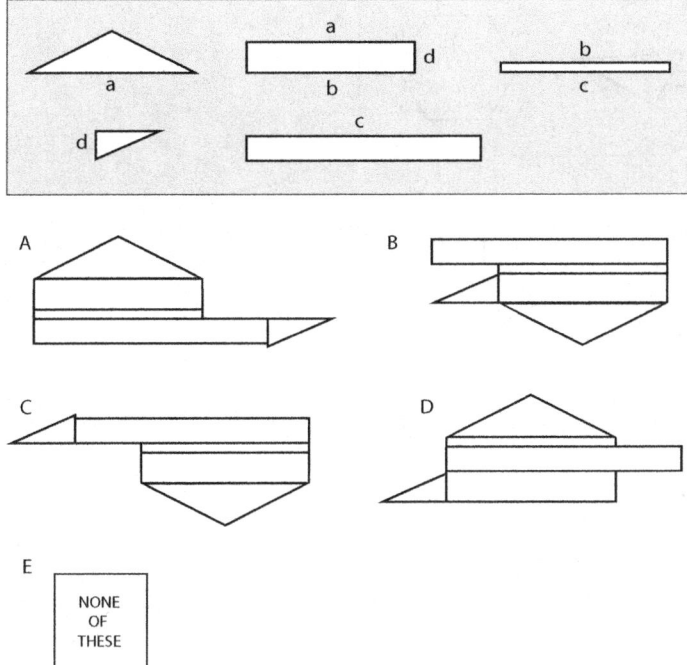

Question 6

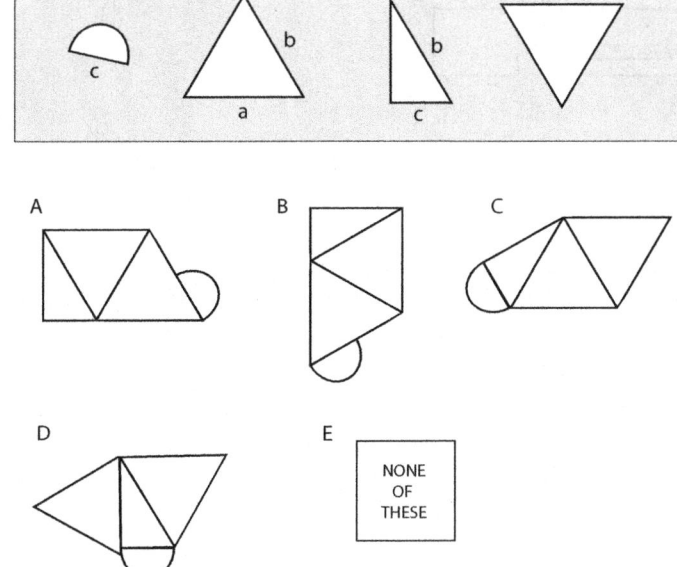

74 Defence Aptitude Assessment

Question 7

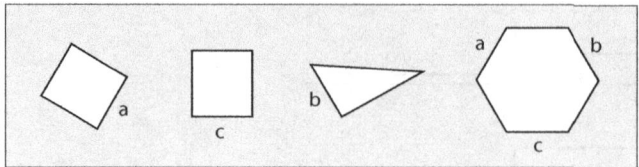

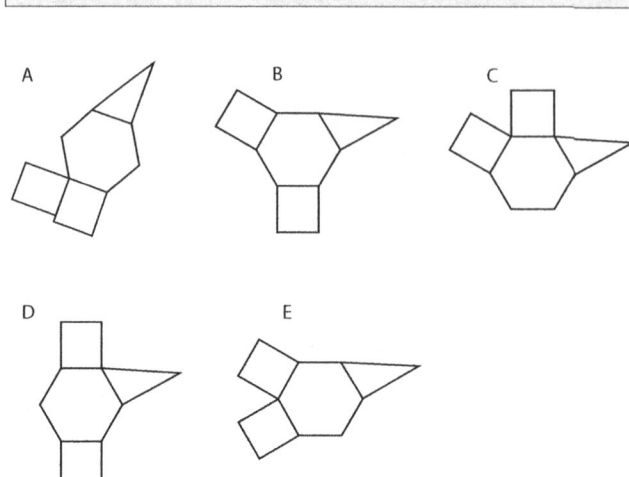

Question 8

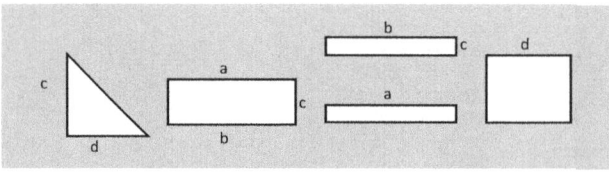

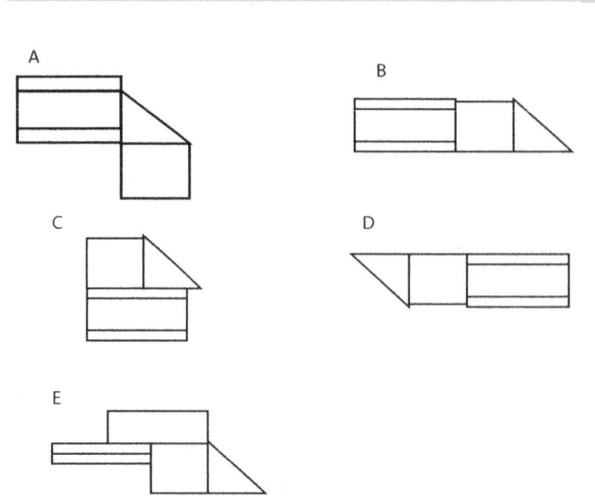

Question 9

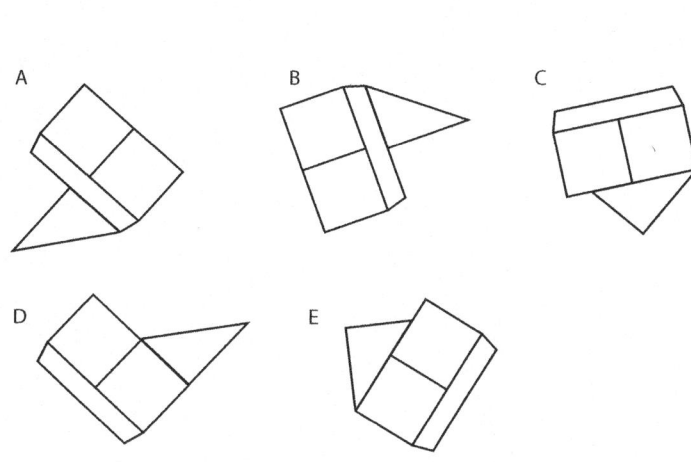

Question 10

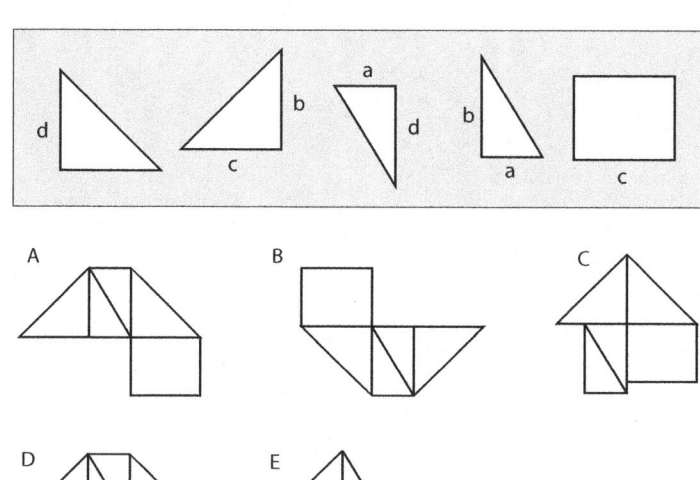

SPATIAL REASONING EXERCISE 1 ANSWERS

Q1. A
Q2. E
Q3. C
Q4. E
Q5. B
Q6. C
Q7. B
Q8. A
Q9. D
Q10. E

Spatial Reasoning Tests

SPATIAL REASONING PRACTICE QUESTION 2

Look at the two objects below.

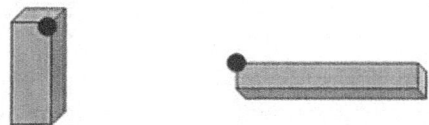

You now have to decide which of the four answer options provided demonstrates both objects rotated with the dot remaining in the SAME corner as found on the original objects.

Look at the answer options below.

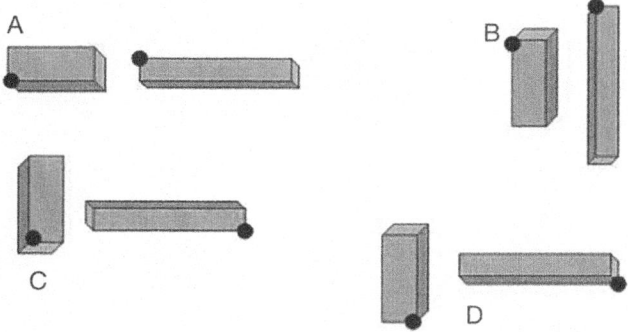

The correct answer is **C**. This is because BOTH objects have been rotated 180°.

Remember, the objects have to rotate EXACTLY the same amount!

78 Defence Aptitude Assessment

SPATIAL REASONING EXERCISE 2

You have 3 minutes to complete the 10 questions.

Question 1

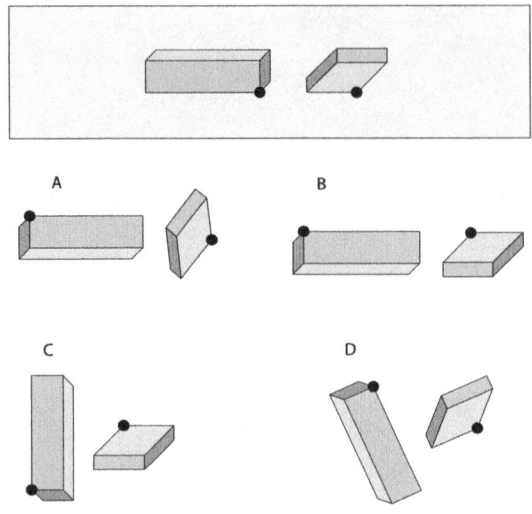

Question 2

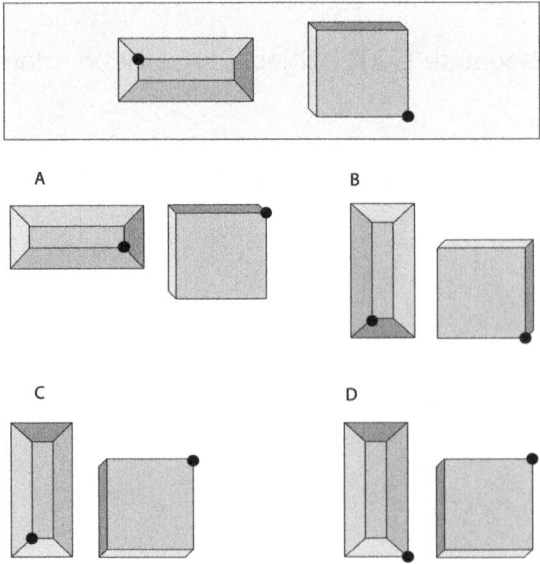

Question 3

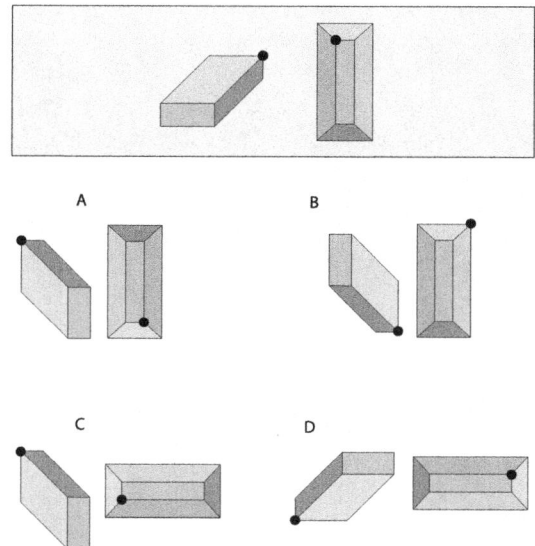

Question 4

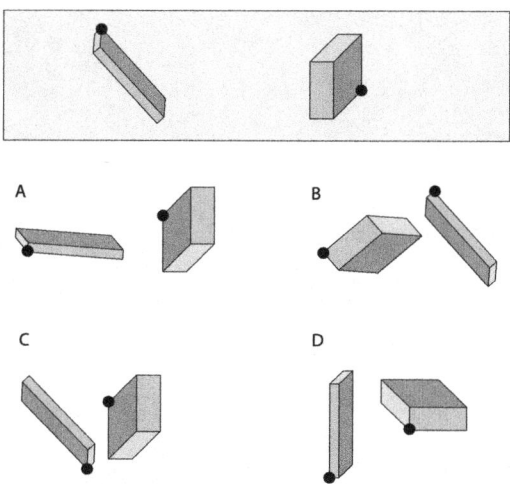

Question 5

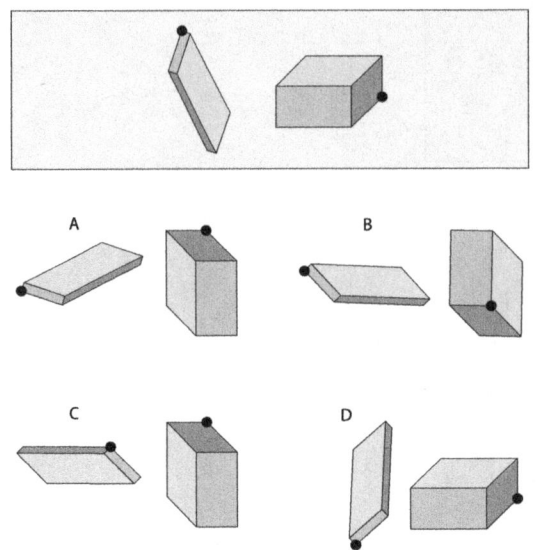

Question 6

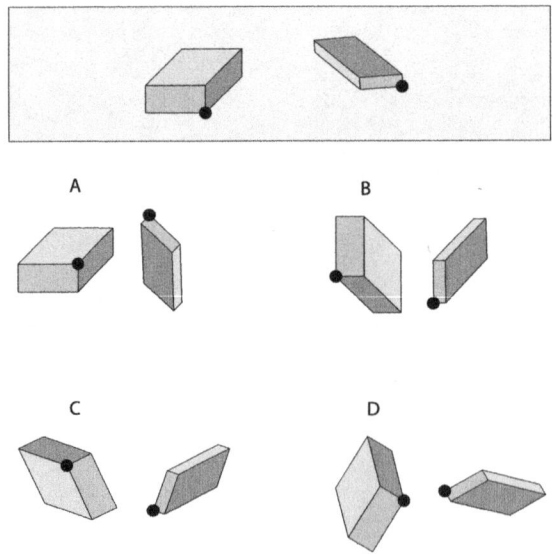

Question 7

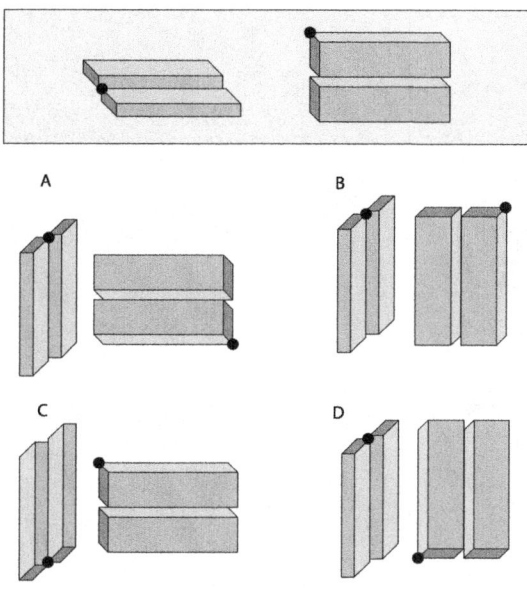

Question 8

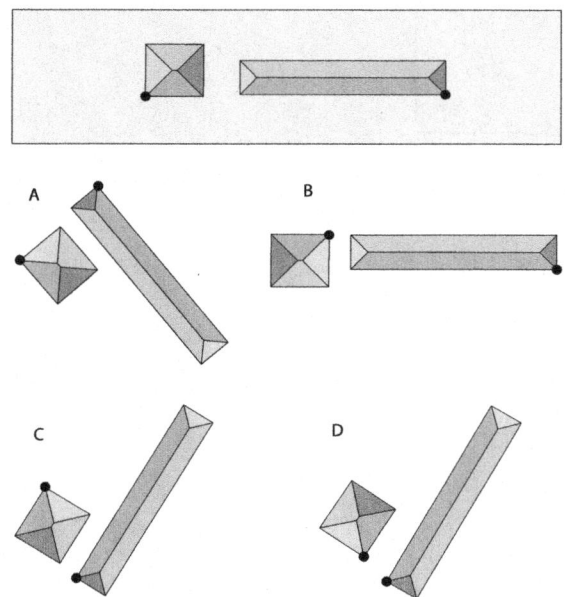

Question 9

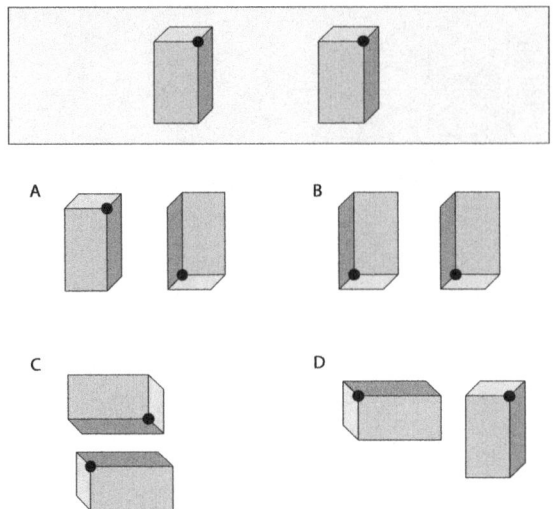

Question 10

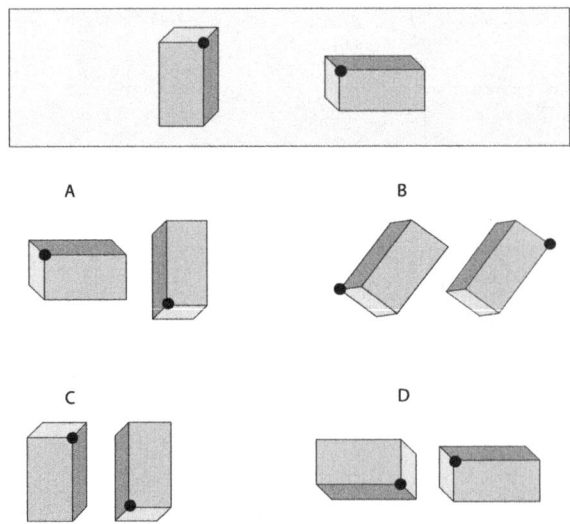

SPATIAL REASONING EXERCISE 2 ANSWERS

Q1. B

Q2. C

Q3. C

Q4. C

Q5. A

Q6. B

Q7. B

Q8. C

Q9. B

Q10. A

Work Rate Tests

86 Defence Aptitude Assessment

During the DAA, you will be required to undertake a Work Rate Test. This form of test assesses your ability to work quickly and accurately whilst carrying out routine tasks; something which is integral to the role in the Royal Navy.

WORK RATE PRACTICE QUESTION

Before we move on to the test questions, let's take a look at a sample question.

To begin with, study the following grid. In the grid, you will be able to see different numbers, letters and symbols.

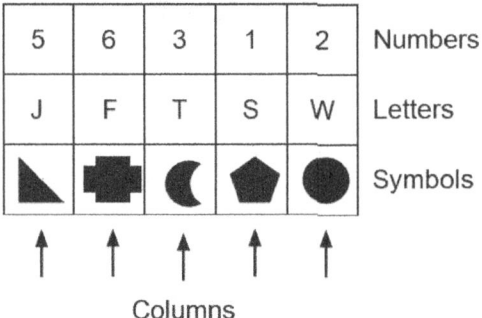

For these questions, you will be given a code consisting of numbers, letters and/or symbols. Your task is to look at the answer options and decide which code has been taken from the **SAME** columns as the original code.

For example, take a look at the following code: **563**

Now look at the five alternatives.

A.	b.	C.	d.	E.
J (2	◣ FT	✚ 51	● 6S	3J2

The question is: which code (A-E) has been taken from the **SAME** columns as the code 563?

You can see that the answer is in fact B. The reason for this is that the code has been taken from the **SAME** columns as the original code of 563.

Work Rate Tests

WORK RATE EXERCISE 1

You have 10 minutes to complete the 10 questions.

Question 1

Which of the answers below is an alternative to the code **4H9**?

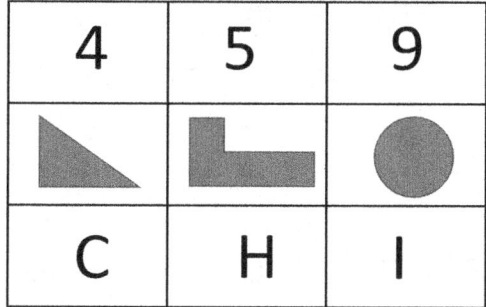

A. C 5 ⌐   B. 4 5 H   C. ●C I   D. C 5 ●

Question 2

Which of the answers below is an alternative to the code **J1X**?

A. ● 9 1   B. 5E9   C. ●⌐1   D. 9 1 ●

Question 3

Which of the answers below is an alternative to the code **7B6**?

U	5	✚
✖	●	B
6	7	V

A. 7 U V   B. U 7 B   C. ●V✖   D. ✖●✚

Question 4

Which of the answers below is an alternative to the code **CB3**?

A	B	C
3	9	✦
▬	■	7

A. A 7 9   B. ▬B✦   C. 3 B ■   D. ✦ 9 A

Question 5

Which of the answers below is an alternative to the code **6EYX**?

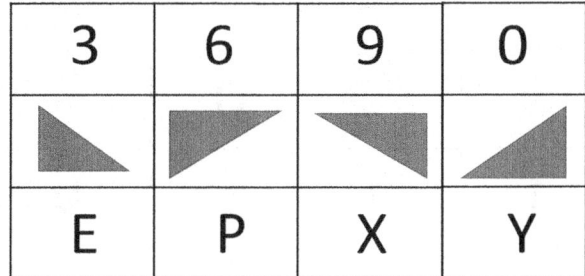

A. 9 0 P ◣   B. ◥ 3 0 9   C. ◣ 6 9 ◢   D. ◣ 6 X ◣

Question 6

Which of the answers below is an alternative to the code **7F8** ⬆ ?

A. 9 ⬇ WK   B. T5KW   C. 57 ⬅ W   D. 9587

Question 7

Which of the answers below is an alternative to the code **Y96R**?

F	Y	I	♥
R	◯	0	9
1	4	◖	6

A. 4691 B. 1◖◯9 C. I♥◖9 D. F◯I♥

Question 8

Which of the answers below is an alternative to the code **5DA**?

R	A	F	S
1	3	5	7
D	◀	B	➡

A. DF3 B. 5S1 C. F1◀ D. 5D➡

Question 9

Which of the answers below is an alternative to the code **GMN**?

T	G	⌐	5
2	◯	N	M
⊘	9	0	F
7	8	X	✥

A. 9N2 **B.** ◯F2 **C.** 9✥X **D.** M9N

Question 10

Which of the answers below is an alternative to the code **PON**?

▶	H	O	5
F	⬆	T	N
8	P	0	✖
4	★	X	1

A. HX1 **B.** ⬆O▶ **C.** ▶⬆O **D.** 1▶O

WORK RATE EXERCISE 1 ANSWERS

Q1. D

Q2. B

Q3. C

Q4. D

Q5. B

Q6. B

Q7. A

Q8. C

Q9. C

Q10. A

Work Rate Tests

WORK RATE EXERCISE 2

You have 10 minutes to complete the 10 questions.

Question 1

Which of the answers below is an alternative to the code **281**?

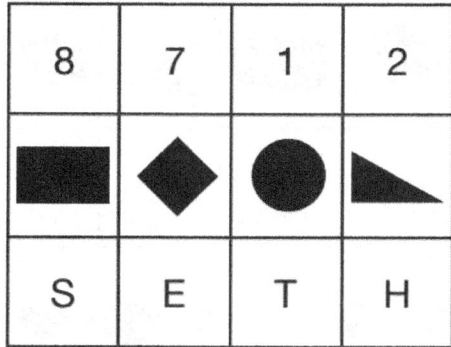

A. 8■E   B. HS●   C. ▲5◆   D. T■H

Question 2

Which of the answers below is an alternative to the code **493**?

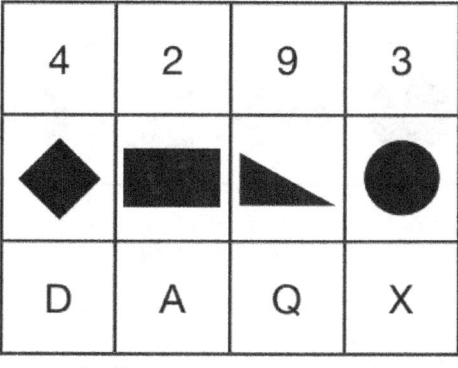

A. D▲X   B. ◆QA   C. ▲AD   D. DAX

Question 3

Which of the answers below is an alternative to the code **987**?

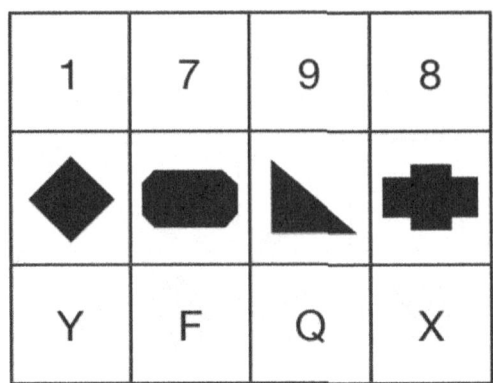

A. F  Y   B. ◆XY   C.  Y◆   D. QX ⬭

Question 4

Which of the answers below is an alternative to the code **135**?

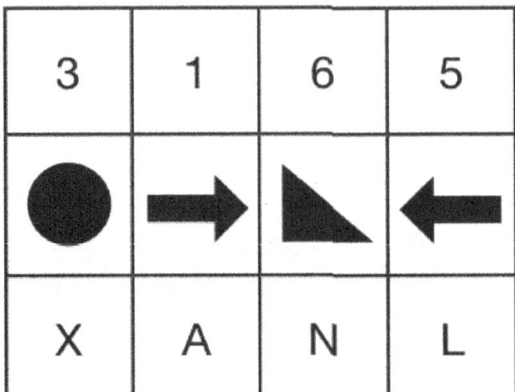

A. A ◣ X   B. ◣ AN   C. ➡ XL   D. ➡ LX

Question 5

Which of the answers below is an alternative to the code **1WR**?

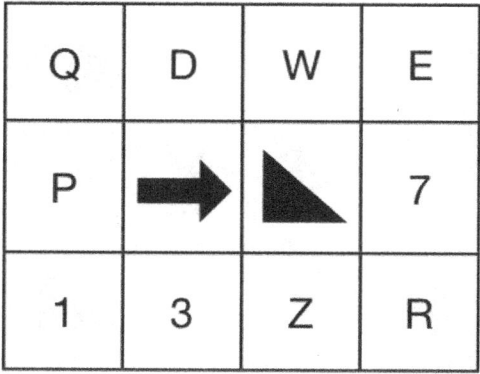

A. PZE **B.** ▲ 17 **C.** ➡ 1R **D.** Q3R

Question 6

Which of the answers below is an alternative to the code **DAE**?

A. Q17 **B.** ↱Q6 **C.** ⬅16 **D.** ERA

Question 7

Which of the answers below is an alternative to the code **326**?

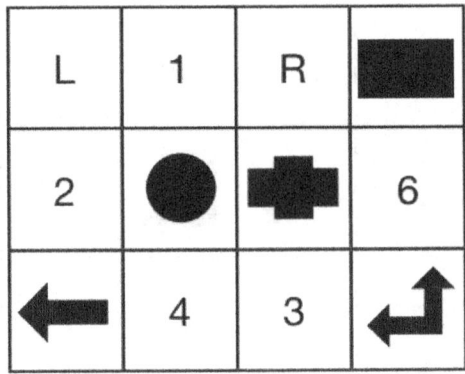

A. RL  **B.** ↰21 **C.** ✚L4 **D.** R62

Question 8

Which of the answers below is an alternative to the code **£4&**?

L	1	R	£
2	9	&	6
=	4	3	>

A. 61> **B.** >9= **C.** >1R **D.** =13

Question 9

Which of the answers below is an alternative to the code **Q3%**?

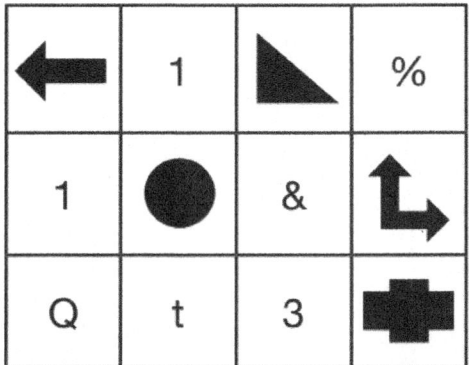

A. 1&    B. 13&   C. t▨1   D. 11&

Question 10

Which of the answers below is an alternative to the code **1>6**?

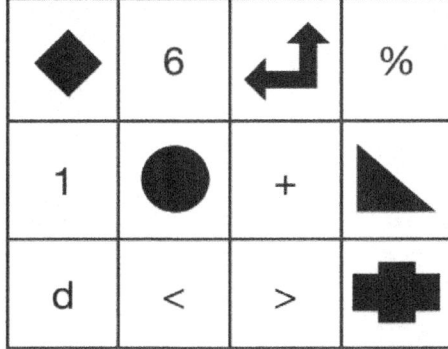

A. +d<   B. d+<   C. ▨d<   D. 1>%

WORK RATE EXERCISE 2 ANSWERS

Q1. B

Q2. A

Q3. D

Q4. C

Q5. A

Q6. C

Q7. A

Q8. C

Q9. A

Q10. B

Mechanical Comprehension

Defence Aptitude Assessment

During the Defence Aptitude Assessment you will be required to sit a Mechanical Comprehension Test.

Mechanical Comprehension Tests are an assessment that measures an individual's ability to learn and understand mechanical concepts.

During the actual Mechanical Comprehension Test with the navy, you will have a specific amount of time to answer each question. Read the questions carefully and then choose the correct answer.

In the real test, there are 20 questions you need to answer. You will be given 10 minutes to complete this assessment.

MECHANICAL COMPREHENSION EXERCISE 1

Q1. Which of the following tools would be most suitable for removing remove spark plugs from an engine?

A	B	C

Q2. From the following gear configuration which gear will rotate at the quickest speed?

A	B	C	D	E
Gear A	Gear B	Gear C	Gear D	All the same

Q3. When pulling a nail from a plank of timber, what type of lever is demonstrated?

A	B	C
Class 2	Class 3	Class 1

Q4. Which of the following screws/bolts are least likely to round/strip the head and provide a greater torque?

A	B	C	D

Q5. What is the function of a 'resistor' in electrical comprehension?

A	B	C	D
This will change resistance when temperature changes	Is used to store electrical charge	This is used to measure voltage	This will reduce the flow of the current

Q6. Which type of drill heads would be used to create the recessed hole as seen in picture?

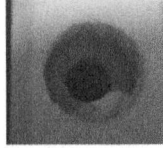

A	B	C	D

Q7. In the following circuit which switches will need to be closed to allow Bulbs B and C to illuminate?

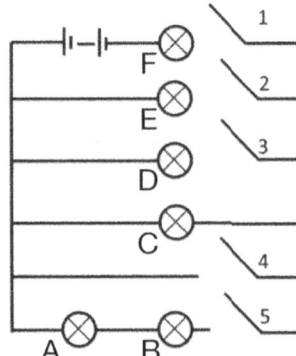

A	B	C	D
All of the switches	Switches 1 & 3	Switches 1, 2 & 4	Switches 1 & 5

Q8. The human arm is an example of a what class lever?

A	B	C
3rd class lever	2nd class lever	1st class lever

Q9. Which part of the human arm is the fulcrum?

A	B	C	D
Wrist	Bicep	Elbow	Forearm

Q10. If I applied force at 29 N, what would be the representative figure in Kgs rounded up to the nearest Kg?

A	B	C	D
4 kgs	3 kgs	5 kgs	7 kgs

Q11. An opening tool is used to pry the lid off a tin of paint. Where is the pivot point during this action?

A	B	C	D
Between the handle of the tool and the hand of the user.	Where the tool rests on the rim of the paint tin.	Under the flat edge at the far end of the tool.	Roughly 15 mm below the handle of the tool.

Q12. Two identical balls are released at the same time down separate ramps which are made of the same material, but have different gradients. Which ball will reach the end first?

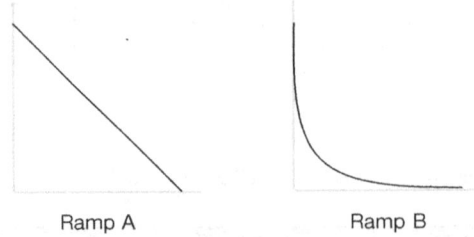

A	B	C
Ramp A	Ramp B	Both balls will reach the end at the same time.

Q13. What is the purpose of a star washer?

A	B	C	D
To increase the bearing surface area of a screw.	To reduce heat and friction when tightening a screw.	To prevent damage to a surface that needs a screw installed and then removed.	To prevent a screw loosening by itself.

Q14. What is the efficiency of this machine, expressed as a percentage?

A	B	C	D
33%	51%	66%	151%

Q15. $W = F \times d$ is the formula for what?

A	B	C	D
Weight	Work done	Extension	Compression

Q16. A car with a mass of 1,200 kg is travelling at a speed of 55 metres per second. What is the momentum of the car?

A	B	C	D
22 kg m/s	1,100 kg m/s	1,200 kg m/s	66,000 kg m/s

Q17. Which of the following is **not** a type of contact force?

A	B	C	D
Friction	Magnetic	Air resistance	Tension

Q18. When a balloon is squeezed, which of the following is true?

A	B	C	D
The volume is decreased & the pressure is increased	The volume is increased & the pressure is decreased	The volume is decreased & the pressure is decreased	The volume is increased & the pressure is increased

Q19. Using the table, work out the cost of electricity bill for the period between the two readings rounded to the nearest whole pence?

Last meter reading	Current meter reading	Cost per unit
58,965 kWh	59,853 kWh	12.45p

A	B	C	D
£686.24	£12.45	£888.00	£110.56

Q20. A force of 15 N is used to turn on a tap.

The perpendicular distance from the pivot is 16 cm.

What is the moment of the force?

A	B	C	D
2.4 Nm	24 Nm	240 Nm	2,400 Nm

Mechanical Comprehension

MECHANICAL COMPREHENSION EXERCISE 1 ANSWERS

1. C
Spark plugs are usually set into a recess in the engine block. You would need a ratchet and socket to remove spark plugs

2. E
As all the cogs have the same amount of teeth and are interlocked, they will move at the same speed.

3. C
Class 1 lever. When pulling a nail, the nail is the Load, the Fulcrum is the head of the hammer, and the Force or effort is at the other end of the handle, which is the Beam.

4. C
The star drive provides the best torque and will be least likely to strip the screw head.

5. D
A resistor reduces the flow of an electrical current.

6. B
This is a flat wood drill bit which would create the hole shown in the image.

7. D
To allow bulbs B and C to illuminate switches 1 and 5 need to be closed.

8. A
The human arm is an example of a 3rd class lever. The fulcrum is between the effort and load.

9. C
The elbow acts as the fulcrum in the human arm.

10. B
3 kgs is the correct answer 1 kg = 9.81 N
29 ÷ 9.81 = 2.956 kgs rounded to the nearest kg = 3 kgs.

11. B
When prying the lid off a tin of paint, the lid is the load, the effort is created by the pushing down on the handle of the tool and the pivot point is where the tool and paint tin meet.

12. B
Ramp B is a brachistochrone curve which means, due to gravity it will reach the end point in the fastest time.

13. D
The 'teeth' on a star washer prevent a screw from loosening by itself by resisting torque.

14. C
Efficiency = input / output. This can be expressed as a percentage by multiplying the answer by 100.
250 / 165 × 100 = 66%

15. B
Work done = force × distance

16. D
Momentum = mass × velocity
Momentum = 1,200 × 55 = 66,000 kg m/s

17. B
Magnetic force is the only non-contact force from the options given.

18. A
When a balloon is squeezed, the volume is decreased as there is less space for the gas particles to occupy and as the gas particles are closer together they will collide more so the pressure is increased.

19. D
59,853 - 58,965 × 12.45 = 11,055.6

20. A
15 L 0.16 = 2.4 Nm

Mechanical Comprehension

MECHANICAL COMPREHENSION EXERCISE 2

Q1. How many bulbs will illuminate in the following circuit?

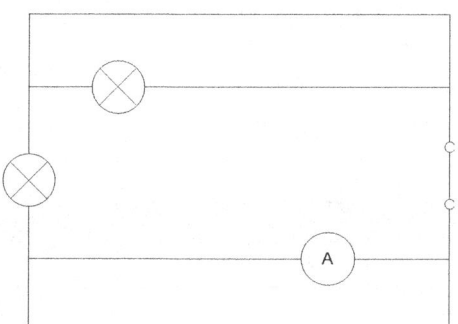

A	B	C	D
No bulbs	One bulb	Two bulbs	Three bulbs

Q2. The diameter of wheel A is 40% bigger than wheel B's. If wheel A rotates in a clockwise motion at 40 rpm, at what speed and direction will wheel B rotate at?

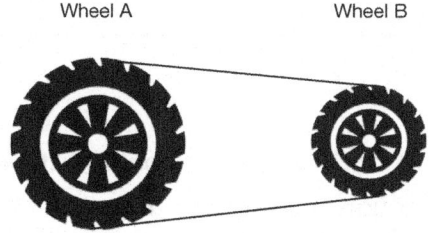

NOT TO SCALE

A	B	C	D
40 rpm clockwise	56 rpm clockwise	100 rpm clockwise	100 rpm anti-clockwise

Q3. $V = IR$ is the formula for what?

A	B	C	D
Voltage	Ohm's Law	Volume	Power

Q4. How many sets of magnets will be magnetised together?

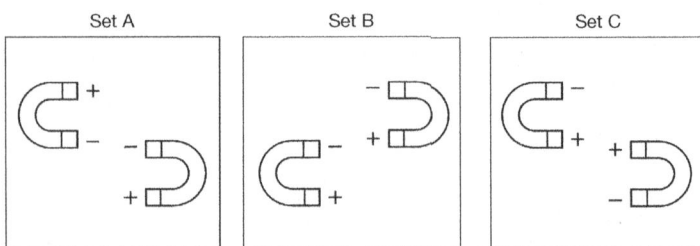

A	B	C	D
No sets	All sets	Set B only	Set C only

Q5. Which shape can be created by folding the given net?

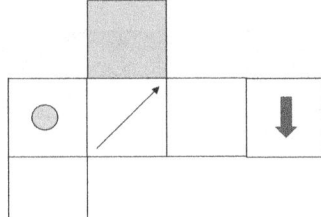

A	B	C	D

Q6. Gears M, N, O, P and Q are interlocked. If gear O is rotating anti-clockwise, in what direction is gear Q rotating?

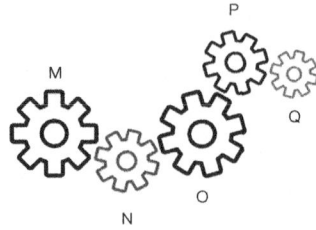

A	B	C	D
Clockwise	Anti-clockwise	It isn't rotating	It rotates in alternative directions

Mechanical Comprehension

Q7. The scale is 1:20,000. A distance measures 5 cm on the map, what is the actual distance?

A	B	C	D
4 km	10 km	25 km	100 km

Q8. What amount of work is required to move the weight below, a distance of 8 metres?

32 N

A	B	C	D
4 J	24 J	40 J	256 J

Q9. If a storm producing thunder and lightning is approaching your local area.

Do you hear it, or see it first?

A	B	C	D
Hear it first	Hear it and see it at the same time	See it first	Smell it first

Q10. A car is being tested for it's acceleration performance. The car must accelerate from 0 mph up to 60 mph. The time it takes for this to happen is calculated by the distance travelled. Which scenario would take the shortest amount of time?

Scenario A

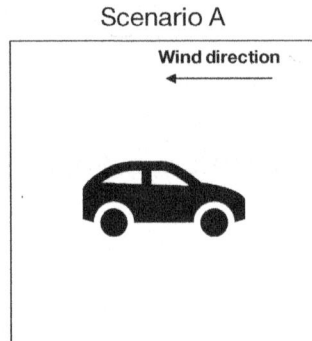

Scenario B

Scenario C

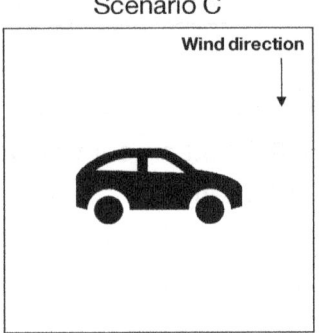

A	B	C	D
Scenario A	Scenario B	Scenario C	All scenarios will take the same amount of time

Q11. How much weight is required to balance point X?

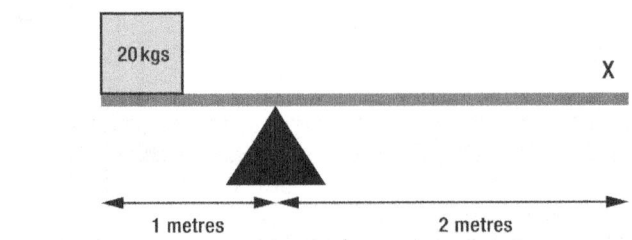

A	B	C	D
5 kg	10 kg	15 kg	20 kg

Mechanical Comprehension

Q12. Two cars are travelling in opposite directions. One of the cars is travelling at a speed of 45 m/s and the other car is travelling at a speed of 30 m/s.

What is their relative speed?

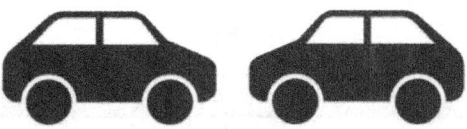

A	B	C	D
60 m/s	45 m/s	30 m/s	75 m/s

Q13. Which pendulum will swing at the fastest speed rate?

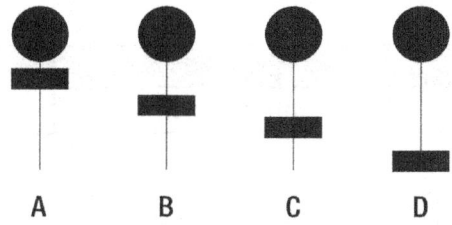

A	B	C	D
Pendulum A	Pendulum B	Pendulum C	Pendulum D

Q14. What is the mechanical advantage?

A	B	C	D
1	2	3	4

Q15. What is the mechanical advantage?

A	B	C	D
1	2	3	4

Q16. If rope A is pulled in the direction of the arrow, which way will wheel C turn?

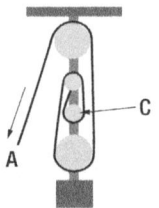

A	B	C
Clockwise	Anti-clockwise	It will not turn

Q17. Which pulley system is a moveable pulley system?

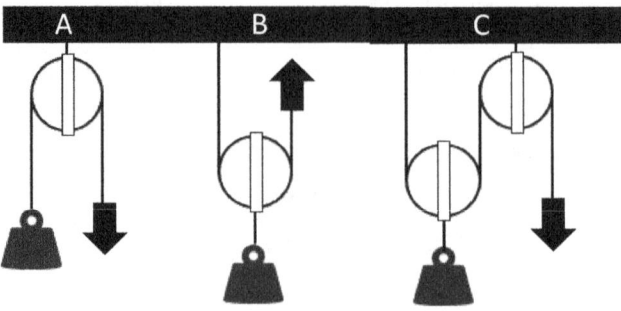

A	B	C
Pulley A	Pulley B	Pulley C

Mechanical Comprehension

Q18. A lift is most similar to which of the following mechanical devices?

A	B	C	D
Spring	Hydraulic jet	Lever	Crane

Q19. Which tank will not empty?

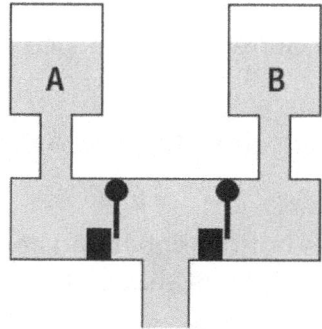

A	B	C	D
Tank A	Tank B	Both tanks will empty	Neither tank will empty

Q20. How much force is required to hold the weight in its current position?

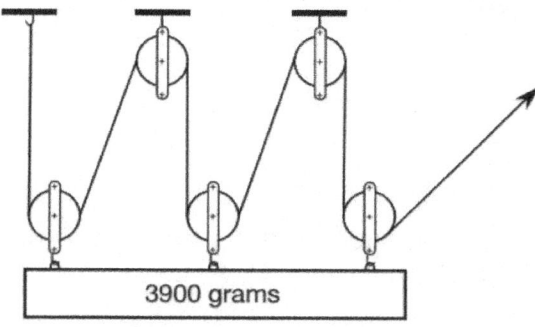

A	B	C	D
800 g	23,400 g	500 g	650 g

MECHANICAL COMPREHENSION EXERCISE 2 ANSWERS

1. A
No bulbs. There is no source of power to the circuit, therefore no bulbs will illuminate.

2. B
56 rpm. Multiply 40 rpm by 1.40 to account for wheel A's diameter being 40% larger than wheel B's.

3. B
Ohm's Law. Voltage = Current × Resistance.

4. C
Set B only. Magnets with opposite poles will be magnetised together.

5. D
The arrow points to the bottom right hand corner, the grey face is to the right of the arrow and the dot is shaded in above the arrow.

6. B
Gear Q will turn anti-clockwise.

7. D
20,000 × 5 = 100,000   100,000 / 1,000 = 100 km

8. D
256 J. 32 N (force) × 8 meters (distance) = 256 J (work done)

9. C
See it first. The speed of light is faster than the speed of sound.

10. B
Scenario B. This scenario will take the shortest amount of time as the wind direction will aid the acceleration speed of the car.

11. B
Point X is twice the distance from the balance point; therefore, half the weight is required. The answer is B, 10 kg.

12. D
The relative speed of the two cars is 45 m/s + 30 m/s = 75 m/s

Mechanical Comprehension

13. A

Pendulum A will swing the fastest speed rate. The lower down the weight, the slower the pendulum will swing.

14. C

The mechanical advantage of this pulley system is 3. There are three supporting ropes.

15. D

The mechanical advantage of this pulley system is 4. There are four supporting ropes.

16. B

Wheel C will rotate anti-clockwise if rope A is pulled in the direction shown.

17. B

Pulley system B is a moveable pulley system.

18. D

A crane is similar to a lift in terms of mechanical function.

19. B

Tank B will not empty because the valve will not permit water to flow past it.

20. D

The weight of the object is 3,900 grams (39 kg). There are 6 sections supporting the weight.

3,900 ÷ 6 = 650 grams

Electrical Comprehension

During the DAA, you will be required to sit an Electrical Comprehension Test.

The test itself is designed to assess your ability to work with different electrical concepts.

During the actual Electrical Comprehension Test with the Royal Navy, you will have a specific amount of time to answer each question. Read the questions carefully and then choose the correct answer.

In the real test, there are 21 questions you need to answer. You will be given 11 minutes to complete this assessment.

Electrical Comprehension

ELECTRICAL COMPREHENSION EXERCISE

You have 11 minutes to complete the 21 questions.

Question 1

In the following circuit, if switch A closes, and switch B remains open, what will happen?

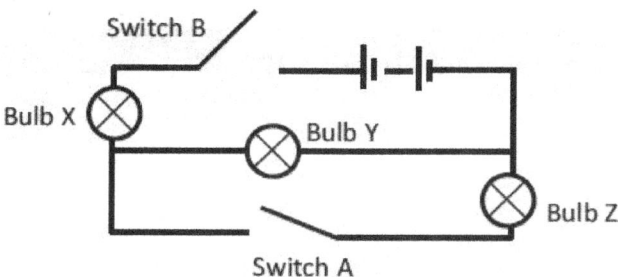

A = Bulbs X, Y, and Z will illuminate.

B = Bulb X will illuminate only.

C = Bulbs Y and Z will illuminate.

D = No bulbs will illuminate.

Question 2

A bicycle uses a battery operated light for its front and rear lights. The front and rear lights are often of different sized bulbs. The filament in the rear lamp has a resistance of 4 ohms. It takes a current of 0.3A. What voltage does the lamp work at?

A	B	C	D
1.8V	0.075V	0.7V	1.2V

Question 3

What will be the voltage at point A, if the battery is 12 volts?

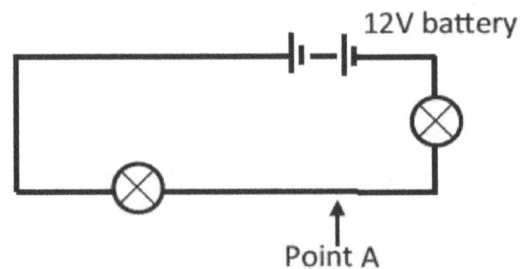

A	B	C	D
0 volts	3 volts	12 volts	6 volts

Question 4

An atom's atomic number is determined by the number of what?

A	B	C	D
Neutrons	Protons	Electrons	Atoms

Question 5

In the following electrical circuit, if switch B closes, what will happen?

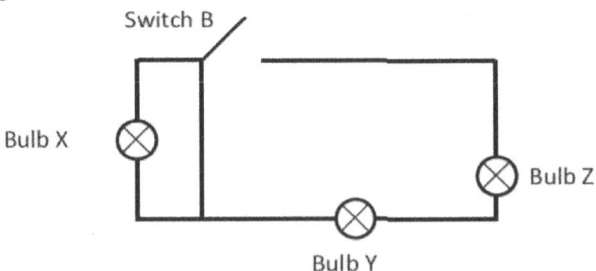

A	B	C	D
Bulbs X, Y and Z will illuminate	Bulb X will illuminate	Bulbs Y and Z will illuminate	No bulbs will illuminate

Question 6

Ammeters measure the amount of current in a circuit. In the circuit below, all of the ammeters are identical. If ammeter A1 reads 0.8A, what will ammeter A3 read?

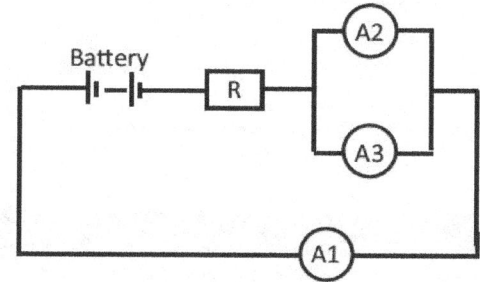

A	B	C	D
0.12A	0.8A	0.4A	0.24A

Question 7

What happens when an electrical charge flows through a resistor?

A = The temperature decreases.

B = The temperature increases.

C = The temperature fluctuates.

D = The temperature stays the same.

Question 8

What is the current in the circuit below?

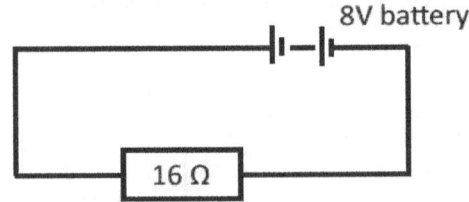

A	B	C	D
2A	1.2A	0.5A	8A

Question 9

Insert the two missing words:

Voltage is a measure of the difference in _____ _____ between two parts of a circuit. The bigger the difference in energy, the bigger the voltage.

A = Electrical current

B = Flowing amperes

C = Concurrent electricity

D = Electrical energy

Question 10

In the following circuit, how many bulbs will illuminate if switches 1 and 5 close?

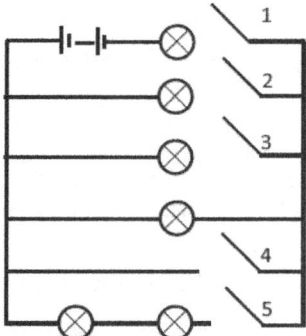

A	B	C	D
2	3	4	5

Question 11

Insert the two missing words:

At a low temperature, the resistance of a thermistor _____ is and allows for _____ current to flow through.

A = High, little.

B = Low, little.

C = High, more.

D = Low, more.

Question 12

Computer monitors and television screens are often covered in dust because...

A = The dust is attracted by the cool air of the technological device.

B = Dust is unmanageable.

C = The dust is attracted to the microfibres of the screen.

D = The dust is attracted by the static charges compelling from the technological device.

Question 13

What is the voltage across the battery?

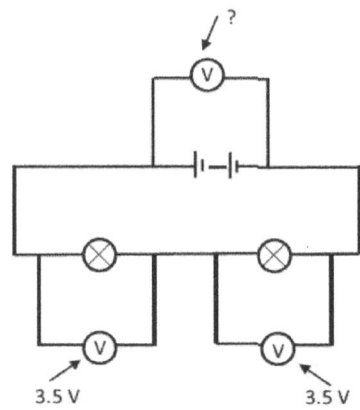

A	B	C	D
3.5V	12.25V	7V	1.25V

Electrical Comprehension

Question 14

Insert the two missing words:

Current is a measure of how much _____ _____ flows through a circuit. The more charge that flows, the bigger the current.

A = Electrical energy.

B = Electrical current.

C = Flowing amperes.

D = Electrical charge.

Question 15

Which of these diagrams of the ammeters is connected correctly?

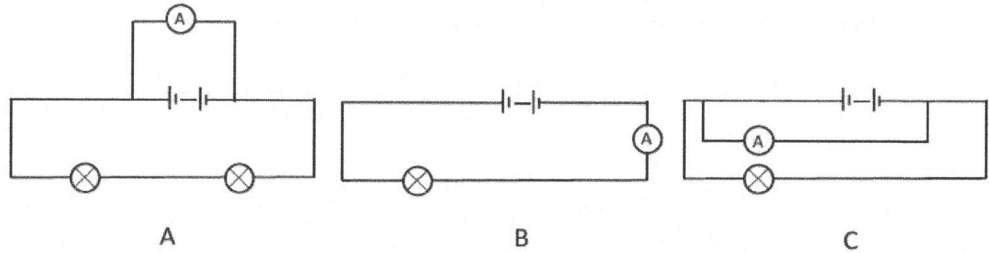

A	B	C
Diagram A	Diagram B	Diagram C

Question 16

In the circuit below, if one bulb blows, what would happen to the other bulbs in the circuit?

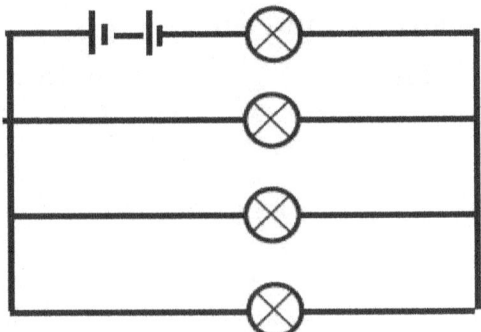

A	B	C	D
Stay lit, but dims	Stay lit, with same brightness	Stay lit, and brightens	No bulbs will illuminate

Question 17

Which of the following statements is true in relation to parallel circuits?

A = The resistance is shared between each of the components connected in parallel of the circuit.

B = The voltage is shared between each of the components connected in parallel of the circuit.

C = The current is shared between each of the components connected in parallel of the circuit.

D = None of the above.

Question 18

Electrical potential difference also means _____.

A = Current

B = Resistance

C = Voltage

D = Parallel circuit

Question 19

What does a transformer do to electrical currents?

A = Changes the voltage.

B = It turns electricity into power.

C = It adds more watts.

D = It conducts heat from the transformer component.

Question 20

Which electrical component is the following a description of?

A safety device which will blow, i.e. 'melt', if the current through it exceeds a specified value.

A	B	C	D
Battery	Fuse	Switch	Resistor

Question 21

When an aeroplane is being refuelled, to avoid causing a spark which could build up from static charge...

A = The person pouring in the fuel needs to pour it in slowly.

B = The aeroplane has rubber tyres which insulates the charges.

C = The refuelling tank and the aeroplane itself are earthed.

D = The person pouring in the fuel needs to pour it in fast.

E = The person needs to be electronically uncharged.

Electrical Comprehension

ELECTRICAL COMPREHENSION EXERCISE ANSWERS

Q1. D = no bulbs will illuminate

If switch A closes, and switch B remains open, no bulbs will illuminate. Even with switch A being an 'on-switch', the fact that switch B remains open means that the power supply (i.e. the battery) cannot supply the power because the circuit is broken.

Q2. D = 1.2V

In order to work out the voltage, you need to multiply the resistance by the current. So, 4 × 0.3 = 1.2V.

Q3. C = 12 volts

In a series circuit, there is only one path for the current, and therefore that current is the same at all points of the path.

Q4. B = protons

An atomic number is determined by the number of protons in an atom's nucleus.

Q5. D = no bulbs will illuminate

The reason that no bulbs will illuminate is because, and although the switch would become an 'on-switch', there is no power source to generate anything, and therefore the bulbs would not be lit.

Q6. C = 0.4A

If ammeter A1 reads 0.8, then ammeters A2 and A3 will have to share this current, therefore each of these would read 0.4.

Q7. B = the temperature increases

When an electrical charge flows through a resistor, the temperature increases. The resistor gets hot from the electrical charge running through it, therefore increasing the temperature.

Q8. C = 0.5A

The current in this circuit is as follows: 8 ÷ 16 = 0.5A.

Q9. D = electrical energy

The two words that are missing in the sentence are 'electrical energy'. Voltage is a measure of the difference in electrical energy between two parts of a circuit.

Q10. C = 4

If switches 1 and 5 were closed, 4 bulbs would illuminate. The bulb left of switch 1 would illuminate, the two bulbs left of switch 5 would illuminate, and the bulb on the fourth horizontal line would illuminate.

Q11. A = high, little

At a low temperature, the resistance of a thermistor is high, and little current can flow through. In comparison, at a high temperature, the resistance of a thermistor is low, and allows for more current to flow through.

Q12. D = the dust is attracted by the static charges compelling from the technological device

Computer screens and television screens are often covered in dust because the dust becomes attracted by the static charges compelling from the technological device. The electrical element of statics can be demonstrated when two objects rub together and become 'electronically charged'. When you remove the dust, you often hear the static electricity 'snapping'.

Q13. C = 7V

The circuit contains two elements that share the voltage. Therefore, the overall voltage of the battery is as follows: 3.5 + 3.5 = 7V.

Q14. D = electrical charge

In order for the sentence to make sense, the two words that you would need to enter into the sentence are 'electrical charge'. So, the sentence would read 'current is a measure of how much electrical charge flows through a circuit. The more charge that flows, the bigger the current'.

Q15. B = diagram B

Diagram B is wired correctly because ammeters need to be wired in a series circuit. The ammeter needs to be connected by one path of wiring.

Q16. B = stay lit, with same brightness

If one of the bulbs goes out, it does not affect the other bulbs. The bulbs are all placed on different paths which are linked by the same battery. Therefore, if one path stops working, the others will continue to work. This does not affect the brightness of the bulbs as the bulbs are still powered by the same amount of power from the battery.

Q17. C = the current is shared between each of the components connected in parallel of the circuit.

Within a parallel circuit, the current is shared amongst each component that is connected in parallel.

Q18. C = voltage

Electrical potential difference is also the same as voltage. Voltage can be defined as measuring the difference in electrical energy.

Q19. A = changes the voltage

A transformer component within an electrical circuit is a device whereby it transfers energy between two or more circuits. With an alternating current, a transformer will increase or decrease the voltage as it makes the transfer.

Q20. B = fuse

A fuse can be used as a safety device which will blow, i.e. melt, if the current through it exceeds a specified value. A fuse consists of a strip of wire that melts/breaks an electrical circuit when the current is deemed to be at an unsafe level.

Q21. C = the refuelling tank and the aeroplane itself are earthed

When a tank of an aeroplane is being refuelled, the refuelling tank and the aeroplane are earthed. A bonding line is used to earth the aeroplane before it is refuelled, in order to ensure that it is safe to add fuel to the aircraft's tank.

A Few Final Words

You have now reached the end of your Royal Navy Defence Aptitude Assessment book. Now, you should feel more confident and capable of tackling your Royal Navy DAA. We hope you have found this guide an invaluable insight into the type of test you will face during the application process of joining the Royal Navy.

For any psychometric test, there are a few things to remember to help you perform at your best…

REMEMBER – The THREE Ps!

1. **Prepare.** This may seem relatively obvious, but you will be surprised by how many people fail psychometric testing because they lacked knowledge and understanding of what to expect. Be sure to practise these tests before having to sit your real test. Not only will you become familiar with the testing questions, it will also take off some of the pressure leading up to that all important test. Like anything, the more you practise, the more likely you are to succeed!

2. **Perseverance.** Everybody comes across setbacks in their life, or times when there are obstacles in the way of their goals. The important thing to remember when this happens, is to use those setbacks and obstacles as a way of progressing. It is what you do with your past experiences that helps to determine your success in the future. If you fail at something, consider 'why' you have failed. This will allow you to improve and enhance your performance for next time.

3. **Performance.** Your performance will determine whether or not you are likely to succeed. Attributes that are often associated with performance are self-belief, motivation and commitment. Self-belief is important for anything you do in your life. It allows you to recognise your own abilities and skills and believe that you can do well. Believing that you can do well is half the battle! Being fully motivated and committed is often difficult for some people, but we can assure you that nothing is gained without hard work and determination. If you want to succeed, you will need to put in that extra time and hard work!

Work hard, stay focused, and achieve your dream career!

Good luck with your Royal Navy Defence Aptitude Assessment. We wish you the best of luck with all your future endeavours!

The how2become team

The How2Become Team

FOR MORE CAREERS GUIDANCE GO TO:

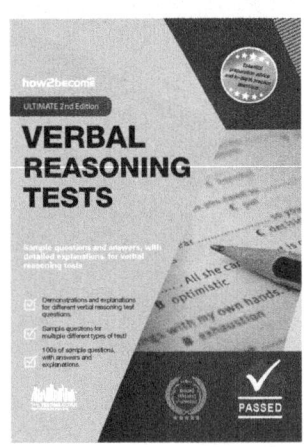

WWW.HOW2BECOME.COM

Get Access To

FREE

Psychometric Tests

www.MyPsychometricTests.co.uk

Made in the USA
Monee, IL
03 May 2026

49438377R00077